PINEWOOD

PINEWOOD

THE STORY OF AN ICONIC STUDIO

Bob McCabe

preface

CONTENTS

1. Pinewood at 80   8

2. Where It All Began   54

3. Shepperton Flickers into Frame   84

4. All This, and World War II   96

5. After the War – Up and Rolling Again   110

6. The Name's Bond   158

7. Meanwhile, Over at Shepperton, a Man Named Stanley Kubrick   184

8. A New Stage   196

9. Look, Up in the Sky   228

10. Shepperton Gets an Alien of Their Own   244

11. Building Character   262

12. Time for a New Hero   284

13. Many Happy Returns   298

14. The Shape of Things to Come   336

Bibliography   364

Index   365

Acknowledgements   372

Author's Note   373

Image Credits   374

PINEWOOD AT 80

FOR OVER EIGHTY YEARS, Pinewood Studios have made dreams a reality. In that time they have hosted super-spies and superheroes, they have seen the *Titanic* sink and the British film industry both fall and rise. They have taken us to a galaxy far, far away and to the streets we all walk every day. They have made the world laugh and cry in equal measure, and have been there as the careers have unfolded for some of the biggest movie stars and greatest film-makers of all time. The odds are Pinewood, alongside its fellow studio Shepperton – initially a rival, now a sister – has played a part in the memories of just about anyone who has ever set foot inside a cinema.

After all, memories are what these studios have been producing for the past eighty years.

The last few years have seen Pinewood Studios expand both overseas and at home, playing host to the biggest films of the day. From Bond to Universal to Marvel to *Star Wars*, Pinewood has become the destination of choice throughout the film-making community worldwide.

'I've made movies since the early '80s in the UK,' explains Kathleen Kennedy, president of Lucasfilm and producer of (amongst many others) *Star Wars: The Force Awakens*, 'so there's a long history and an association that we have, beginning with the *Indiana Jones* movies. Obviously, with George Lucas being the executive producer on those films, I was acutely aware of what he thought about the talent base in the UK, and it's been a growing industry here ever since.'

'So I have this past history of working in the UK and always considered Pinewood the gold standard, even though I had actually never worked there. I visited before – Frank Marshall, my husband, actually did the early Bourne movie there – and we often talked about working at Pinewood. But I have to say, once we got on the Pinewood lot and began to set up the first film, it became very clear that this was where we hoped to set up a base of operations.'

From *Star Wars: The Force Awakens* to *Avengers: Age of Ultron*, from *The Dark Knight* to *Skyfall*, from going into space with *Gravity* to going into the woods with *Into the Woods*, from *Cinderella* to *Captain America: Civil War* – the films that have shot at Pinewood's group of studios in recent times reflect the biggest successes at the global box office in the current millennium.

Film-makers choose Pinewood for the simple reason that it meets all of their needs, and more.

One of the key reasons for this ongoing success was a decision taken by then-new studio runners Michael Grade and Ivan Dunleavy back at the turn of the century. The notion was to combine Pinewood with its largest and longest-standing competitor, Shepperton Studios, at that time run by a team headed by film-making brothers Ridley and Tony Scott, aided by their hands-on adviser Neville Shulman. It was a notion that Ridley Scott firmly agreed with. 'The studio business was very competitive,' the director recalls, 'mostly with Pinewood in our case. I strongly felt that Shepperton must have a partner studio to benefit the marketplace. We finally came together, creating the busiest film studio community in the world.'

It was a historic move, and by 2001, the merger was a reality, and the face of the British film industry had changed forever.

J. J. Abrams with Harrison Ford on the set of *Star Wars: The Force Awakens*.

PRECEDING PAGE: When the *Star Wars* franchise was brought back to the big screen by Disney and J. J. Abrams, they based their new adventures not in a galaxy far, far away – but in Iver Heath, Buckinghamshire, at Pinewood Studios, for *Star Wars: The Force Awakens* in 2015.

'The model I'd been looking at was the 1978 *Superman*, that Richard Donner made. They did a certain amount of location shooting in New York for that film, but everything else was done over here at Pinewood Studios.'
Christopher Nolan on bringing Bruce Wayne back home for *Batman Begins*

Director Tim Burton has spent many years building his hugely imaginative worlds on the famed 007 Stage – here we see him directing the Oompa Loompas during filming for his take on the confectionary-based world of Willy Wonka in the 2005 adaptation of Roald Dahl's *Charlie and the Chocolate Factory*.

In retrospect, this step of combining Pinewood with Shepperton seemed like a natural choice. 'Shepperton had been Pinewood's "arch-rival" since the 1930s and they were the two great studios of the UK,' explains CEO Ivan Dunleavy. 'The logic was to put one and one together and hope to come out with three.'

At a time when film production in the UK was on the upturn but by no means guaranteed, it was a bold move.

Both studios were doing well together in the early 2000s, with on going relationships with such productions companies as the UK's own Working Title, seeing stages going to the likes of *Bridget Jones's Diary*, *About a Boy* and *Love Actually*, and board member Tony Scott bringing his Robert Redford–Brad Pitt starrer *Spy Game* back to Shepperton. As well as welcoming back Pinewood's longest-standing client, the James Bond series, with *Die Another Day*, Pierce Brosnan's final outing as 007, alongside such Pinewood perennials as Tim Burton, who once again based his take on Roald Dahl's *Charlie and the Chocolate Factory* at his studio of choice.

Another favoured son of both studios, Kenneth Branagh, welcomed the advantages of having them united. Branagh had begun his film-making career at Shepperton in 1989 with *Henry V*, and would continue to return to his preferred stomping ground, including bringing in such large-scale productions as Disney's lavish live-action retelling of *Cinderella* to Pinewood in 2015.

Now there was an opportunity to give film-makers – both old and new – something more than before: the combination of both studios, a situation that could, literally, cover the needs of just about anything.

One of the first to take advantage of this new film-making situation was visionary British director Christopher Nolan. Years before in 1989, Tim Burton had reinvented the screen image of Batman at Pinewood Studios. And now, in 2008, the Dark Knight was ripe for reinvention once more. And Nolan, on a roll from his hugely applauded third film, *Memento*, was the man who took the Batcave to Shepperton (where he spent many an hour jumping a two-and-a-half-tonne Batmobile through a studio-built waterfall).

'The model I'd been looking at, that I first discussed with Warner Brothers, was the

Christian Bale's disturbed yet defiant Batman, as reimagined by Christopher Nolan in *Batman Begins* (2005), the first of his genre-defining Dark Knight Trilogy.

Pinewood has helped move mountains with Everest recreated on the 007 Stage for the vertigo-inducing 2015 mountain-climbing drama of the same name.

1978 *Superman*, that Richard Donner made,' Nolan said on the film's initial release, citing Pinewood's history with superhero movies (something that was only to grow in the coming years). 'They did a certain amount of location shooting in New York for that film, but everything else was done over here at Pinewood Studios. So we created a model of the idea of shooting at Shepperton Studios … I was looking back to a great era of blockbuster film-making from the late '70s where, I think, Hollywood films were doing some really marvellous escapist entertainment on a grand scale. All of those films were done over here in the UK, *Raiders of the Lost Ark*, the first *Star Wars*, *Superman* etc. So for me, it was a fairly natural notion to just look at that model of doing things.'

The film-maker would continue his association with the newly joined studios for his subsequent Bat-film, *The Dark Knight*.

At the same time as Christopher Nolan was reinventing one of Pinewood's original superheroes in Batman, the studio's longest-standing client was busy recasting the twentieth century's most iconic spy into a figure suitable for the new millennium.

In 1995 EON producers Michael G. Wilson and Barbara Broccoli had inherited the mantle of the James Bond movies from their father, Cubby Broccoli.

'My sister and I used to go to the studio all the time,' Broccoli now recalls. 'We went to school in Kingston, so on Fridays we used to go to the studio when we finished school or on holidays. It was our country house. Our playground. When my daughter was about four or five years old, so about '96/'97, I brought her out there. We were playing in the gardens of Pinewood and there was a copse of trees, little bushes, and she went running in there and as I went to get her, I suddenly remembered, Oh my God, I remember being her age and being in this place.'

A little CGI magic and you could almost forget you were still in Buckinghamshire.

'We used to go to the studio when we finished school or on holidays. It was our country house. Our playground.'

Bond producer Barbara Broccoli on a childhood spent at Pinewood

'We always think about Pinewood,' says Bond producer Michael G. Wilson of their charge's spiritual home.

'Certainly, we hope to be there within the next couple of years making another movie,' adds Broccoli. 'It is the home of Bond.'

Director Tim Burton sitting alongside frequent leading man Johnny Depp, at one of his favoured filming locales, Pinewood Studios. Here the two confer on one of the sets built for Burton's take on the classic 1960s TV horror-soap *Dark Shadows* (2012), a production that also saw Pinewood's backlot and Paddock Tank converted into a fully realised fishing village.

When the Avengers assemble, they have been known to do so at certain British film studios. Here seen in *Marvel's Avengers: Age of Ultron* (2015).

This is very literally the case for one Bond in particular, one of Pinewood's longest-standing single residents, a man who took all these recent changes and developments at the studio in his stride, Sir Roger Moore.

'I've had an office here since 1970,' says the former 007. 'And whilst I'm not in the country that often, I do make a point of coming in whenever I can to do a little light dusting and hoovering. It's a lovely place to maintain my UK base, and has been and forever will be a constant in my life – and my second home.

'I do make a point of coming in whenever I can to do a little light dusting and hoovering.'
One of Pinewood's longest-standing residents, Sir Roger Moore

'In 1947 the view across the fields on the approach road to Pinewood was broken only by a cluster of tall pine trees,' Sir Roger continues, 'and then as if from nowhere appeared a mock Tudor double-lodge entrance, and a friendly commissionaire. It was just like arriving at a stately home.

'I was then a rather green twenty-year-old lieutenant serving in the Combined Services Entertainment Unit and being tested for the male lead in *The Blue Lagoon*. It marked the beginning of my long association with the studio and now aged eighty-eight, I am one of Pinewood's oldest (and longest-serving) residents, as I moved in during 1970 when I began work on the TV series *The Persuaders!*, and have been paying rent ever since.'

Whilst the studios were still playing host to Bats, Bonds and Aliens, sometimes, they reasoned, that might not be enough.

So Pinewood started to think of expanding overseas. Since 2009 to the present day, Pinewood has built and now operates studios in Canada, Malaysia, the Dominican Republic and, most recently, Atlanta, Georgia, in the US, with plans for even further expansion globally.

'What we've been able to do successfully is to translate Pinewood's experience, and expertise, into a much more global business,' explains Dunleavy. 'We want producers to get exactly the same quality of experience whether they're in Toronto, Atlanta, Malaysia, the Dominican Republic or here in London.'

As well as growing globally, Pinewood were also keen to provide a myriad of services, and perhaps more than any other, it is in water filming that they lead the way.

Numerous productions over the years, from *A Night to Remember* to *Star Wars VII: The Force Awakens*, have made use of the studio's large exterior water tank, known as the Paddock Tank. But since 2005, Pinewood has been in the unique position of offering film-makers the only permanently filled interior water tank in the world, the Underwater Stage. A facility that in recent years has seen Keira Knightley floating in *Atonement*, Captain America fighting his way into a sub and Sandra Bullock being reborn in *Gravity*.

'The actual landing of the spacecraft in *Gravity*, the re-entry of one capsule, took place at a reservoir,' explains the managing director of Diving Services UK, Dave Shaw. 'It came down in the reservoir then sank in the Underwater Stage at Pinewood and then she finally arrives on the surface in the States. All that is quite usual.

'For *Gravity*, we did the actual landing of the re-entry capsule in Horton over near Staines, at the reservoir. So it landed in the reservoir, sunk in the Underwater Stage here at Pinewood, and Sandra Bullock arrived on the surface in Utah in the States. But that's usual.'

Dave Shaw on the logistics of filming a typical water sequence

Sandra Bullock prepares to be born again in the climactic moments of the Oscar-winning *Gravity* (2013) – set in space, but shot at Shepperton and Pinewood's Underwater Stage. The tank today stands half in the ground and half out of the ground. It is 6 metres deep, 20 metres long and 10 metres wide, kept permanently filled at a constant temperature of 32°C.

As Pinewood began to grow, so did the movies it hosted. James Bond hit his fiftieth anniversary with the secret agent's twenty-third movie, *Skyfall*, not only becoming the first of the series to cross the $1 billion mark at the worldwide box office, but also becoming the first to delve deep into the background of the character and bringing in Oscar-winning director Sam Mendes.

'I'd never worked there before. It was my first time,' the director remembers of not only taking on the world's biggest screen icon, but taking him on in his pivotal anniversary year. 'I'm a big believer in studios, and coming out of the theatre I think it's good to make art in a place that has some sort of personality and some sort of a history, because movies can be quite nebulous, quite rootless. It's also very nice to come into work and see evidence that great movies have been made in the place where you're making your movie.'

For the production of *Skyfall*, Mendes and his team found themselves surrounded by the history of Bond and Pinewood both. 'We had our offices for *Skyfall* near Heatherden Hall, and some of the Bond movies were actually shot there in the original building and in the grounds. Then you go and stay a couple of nights a week at Stoke Park, and you're in the place where they shot the *Goldfinger* scene on the golf course. So it feels like there's a real history there. You work in Hollywood

Keira Knightley takes a deep breath whilst filming in the Underwater Stage for *Atonement* (2007). 'One common problem when filming underwater is artistes are frequently required to fall down and away into the murky depths, it gets awkward to do that in reality due to the increase in pressure, for which the artist would need to equalise their ears,' explains Dave Shaw, the managing director of Diving Services UK, based at Pinewood. 'So we pull them sideways, eliminating the pressure increasing. The far end of the tank can be "smoked out" and the artiste pulled towards the smoke so they disappear into the dark. Pulling them sideways does not affect their ears.'

For Daniel Craig's first outing as James Bond in 2006's *Casino Royale*, the famed Paddock Tank at Pinewood was converted into a miniature Venetian piazza – shortly to be sunk.

FOLLOWING PAGE: For Craig's third outing as Bond in 2012's *Skyfall*, he makes his way into a glamorous casino in Macau, gorgeously lit by cameraman Roger Deakins – but in reality an elaborate set constructed on Pinewood's Paddock Tank, seen here in the light of day with Bond producer Michael G. Wilson.

As Marvel's slate of movies became more ambitious, they found that the Pinewood group of worldwide studios offered them the perfect home, wherever they found themselves. Here, Star-Lord makes a run for camera on an alien world, brought to life on a stage at Shepperton for 2014's *Marvel's Guardians of the Galaxy*. Blue screen to be filled in later.

studios, which I have done many times – I've shot on the Warner Bros lot, on the Universal lot, on the Fox lot, on the Sony lot before, but there's a different, specifically British feeling that you get with Pinewood. It makes you feel proud of the British films that have been made there and the photographs that line the hallways. So it was a big deal for me, and I found it very inspiring.

'When you take on a Bond movie, you're also taking on the history of the franchise. You are making your chapter of the Bond myth. But at the same time you're trying to push on into the future and make something new and different and inspire a new generation, so it seemed very appropriate that Pinewood has a foot in both camps. Pinewood is so steeped in the history of all the other movies that have been made in the series. Q Stage was popping up and being built as we were shooting on the 007 Stage, for example, so you are very aware of Bond as you walk around the studio. You're walking through Pinewood and every day you stare up at one of the largest stages in the world, and the largest stage in England, and it says "Albert R. Broccoli's 007 Stage" and you're very aware that you're part of history.

Determined to make his mark on both Bond and Pinewood, Mendes set out to do something that had never been done before – crashing a London tube train into, and indeed all over, the famed 007 Stage in one of *Skyfall*'s most ambitious and memorable moments.

'One of the great traditions of Bond is to do things for real. That generally means building things and not creating them in a computer,' explains Mendes. 'Now that doesn't necessarily mean crashing a real tube train, but if you don't want to do that in a series of CGI suites in Soho then you need to work out how to build it. For that you need the skill set of people who have been doing this for their whole lives, people like Chris Corbould and his special effects department, not to mention the skills of all the workmen at Pinewood. Those guys built three carriages of tube train and ran it on a track through the ceiling of a constructed set with eleven cameras – all of which were remotely controlled, because it was too dangerous for them to be manually operated. Then we held our breath, crossed our fingers and I shouted, "Action." Literally, it was a one-off. There was no way of doing it again.

'One of the things that I love is old-fashioned in-camera trickery,' Mendes continues. 'We cut the tube crash in the movie so that it appears to be eight carriages. But it's actually the same three carriages coming through the same hole over and over again. The 007 Stage is really a stage built for extraordinary sets and extraordinary creations. In the five years I was working on Bond we built the Shanghai skyscraper, we built the underground world that was MI6, we built the Q branch computer division, we built a set for a tube crash, we built Westminster Bridge – at least a large part of Westminster Bridge with a 360-degree surround of night-time London for *Spectre* and we built Blofeld's lair in the desert. So, for me, it's a place of imagination and inspiration and I have great associations with all of those things. They all feel like environments that for me were real, and yet they all happened within that one space.'

'You are very aware of Bond as you walk around Pinewood. You stare up at one of the largest stages in the world, and it says "Albert R. Broccoli's 007 Stage" and you're very aware that you're part of history.'

Skyfall and *Spectre* director Sam Mendes

But, returning to the logistics of using Pinewood to stage such a train crash, Mendes elaborates. 'The truth is that the stage is big but it's not endless,' he explains, in regard to the 007 Stage, 'and one of the things I was concerned about with the crash was that the tube itself was coming downwards at great velocity and that it would actually hit the wall of the stage. And it did! So you see a little jarring right at the end of the tube crash where it all comes to a juddering stop, and that is actually the tube train hitting the wall of the 007 Stage. Any harder and it might have knocked it down. It was an exhilarating event when it happened. You know you've got weeks and months of preparation, months of building, huge amounts of money at stake and one chance at it – and it's over in thirty seconds. There's an enormous amount of adrenaline involved. It was a great day.'

For his second outing as a Bond director, 2015's *Spectre*, Mendes found himself with an altogether more low-key (but equally important) challenge – taking us inside James Bond's home, built on Pinewood's A Stage.

'It was quite tricky,' says the director of constructing one of his movie's more intimate sets. 'Bond is not somebody who spends much time at home, not surprisingly, and he's also not someone that can leave much of a fingerprint. He doesn't really want to. He is a secret agent, after all. So one of the first things Dennis Gassner and I did with that set, was talk to Daniel Craig, because it was almost like a costume fitting for an actor. You can't plonk him down in a place that he feels his character wouldn't live in, so I wanted to make sure that we had a dialogue and got Daniel's insights, and he was very, very helpful. Our first day of shooting on *Spectre* was on that set.'

More than anything, what Mendes appreciated most of working in such an established studio environment was not only the options it offered him, but the magic it could help to create.

'It's rather wonderful that you fly over Macau, for example, and then you cross the water at Pinewood,' he says, referring to Bond's arrival at the casino in *Skyfall*, shot not in China but on Pinewood's artfully staged exterior Paddock Tank.

'You run across the desert and then you open the door and you're in Pinewood,' Mendes continues, laughing with almost boyish enthusiasm. 'You walk through the

'When you take on a Bond movie, you're also taking on the history of the franchise. You're making your chapter of the Bond myth' – director Sam Mendes on Bond, here with Daniel Craig on the set of *Spectre* (2015).

Sam Mendes on the elaborate underground set built on the 007 Stage for *Skyfall* (2012).

Martin Scorsese went back to the
book whilst shooting *Hugo* at both
Pinewood and Shepperton in 2011.

centre of Tangier and then you enter a hotel room that's in Pinewood. You walk up to a building in Shanghai and then you get in an elevator that's in south London and then you go through the office floor of a neon-lit high-rise that's in Pinewood. It's the centre of everything. The way that Bond works, you're governed by the rhythm of shooting at Pinewood – you shoot out and finish a set, then you go off on location for two or three weeks while they put a new set up and take the old one down, and then you come back and you continue shooting at Pinewood. So it is the centre and the heart of everything. You do feel very happy when you've been away, however glamorous the location, to come home and work in a place which is just filled with craftsmen and people working at the top of their game. It feels, despite the rain and the grey clouds, somehow familiar and welcoming.'

Whilst Sam Mendes was bringing Macau, Shanghai and the like to Pinewood, *Harry Potter* producer David Heyman was using Shepperton to go into space. Heyman had made brief use of both Pinewood and Shepperton during the making of his young-wizarding series, before he turned to Shepperton to create his and Alfonso Cuarón's visually ground-breaking and multi-Oscar-winning *Gravity*.

'We shot most of it at Shepperton,' Heyman recalls. 'We created our offices and did all our testing and we had our main stage there with the Lightbox and all our shift-up computer gear. And then at Pinewood we shot in the tank.'

Gravity was several years in the making as Heyman and his director Cuarón scoured the world researching and developing their unique space-set project, in part, simply waiting for film and visual effects technology to develop to the point where Cuarón's vision was filmable. Together with his award-winning director of photography, Emmanuel Lubezki, Cuarón and his crew developed what was termed the Lightbox – into which they thrust the film's stars, Sandra Bullock and George Clooney, and which was housed on a stage at Shepperton.

'The Lightbox is a 9-foot-by-9-foot box made up of LED panels,' Heyman explains. 'The actor would be in the centre of it in a rig and then coming back from that would be a track on which was a two-tonne robot, the same robot they use for making cars. And at the end of that robot arm would be a camera head and a camera. And all of that was linked up with what was in the Lightbox, which served as the lighting for the actors. Then that was linked up and synched up with the rig which they were in which would move them, because ultimately what we realised was that in space there is no gravity so you couldn't hang Sandra or George upside down because their face would betray the real gravity. They were the right way up, the camera was going upside down.

'When Sandra or George were outside in space, all we were filming was the face. Everything else was created in the computer. So the spacesuit, the movement, space itself, everything was done digitally. You can see it on the DVD extras!'

FOLLOWING PAGE: Director Alfonso Cuarón sought to recreate life – and indeed death – in space for his actors Sandra Bullock and George Clooney on a sound stage at Shepperton. His revolutionary approach to visual effects and the ground-breaking camerawork of director of photography Emmanuel Lubezki resulted in numerous Oscar wins for the David Heyman-produced *Gravity* in 2013.

Among the seven Oscars *Gravity* picked up the following year was, naturally, one for such ground-breaking visual effects work.

'In space there is no gravity so you couldn't hang Sandra or George upside down because their faces would betray the real gravity. They were the right way up, the camera was going upside down.'

Producer David Heyman on making life in space 'real'

By the time Pinewood had started to expand overseas, Heyman's other pet project, the *Harry Potter* movies, had very quietly changed the topography of cinema, not just in the UK, but on a global scale. What *Potter* did was to help create the notion of a *series* of films, what rapidly became known as a *universe*. Not simply sequels, but a defined series. *Potter*, in a literary sense and in J. K. Rowling's eyes, was always intended to be seven books long. Producer Heyman from day one knew (if the audiences came) that he was not producing one film but potentially all seven – eight as it turned out. Prior to this, a film would hope for success and then possibly a sequel. *Star Wars* set an almost random template for the trilogy, but now there was no reason to stop if the stories kept flowing.

When Marvel Studios formed and were able to exploit the rights to their characters (having previously granted film licensing rights to other studios with Spider-Man to Sony and the X-Men and others to 20th Century Fox) they picked up this idea and ran with it. Their initial slate of films was based around *Iron Man*, *The Incredible Hulk* and *Captain America*. But all three movies were tagged with what became known as a 'sting' scene after the end titles had rolled, something that was setting up a bigger picture – one that echoed the nature of Marvel Comics itself, the cross-pollinating team-up that was the Avengers. Suddenly movies weren't just one film and – if box office demanded – a sequel; now you could have a whole cinematic universe. Films were now being seen as franchises, and by Marvel's third outing – *Captain America: The First Avenger* – they were looking to the Pinewood Group to accommodate their paradigm-shifting ambitions. It was the start of a beautiful relationship for Pinewood and Marvel with the likes of *Guardians of the Galaxy*, *Avengers: Age of Ultron* and *Doctor Strange* following *Captain America* on to the sound stages of Pinewood and Shepperton. And as Pinewood expanded into the US via their Atlanta base, it was a relationship destined to grow with *Ant-Man*, *Captain America: Civil War* and *Guardians of the Galaxy Vol. 2* making the new American Pinewood their home.

And once this new paradigm proved to be such a success, others were keen to get in on the action. And to make use of the world-class studios that had been involved.

Chris Evans prepares to go to Civil War in *Marvel's Captain America: Civil War* (2016), one of the first movies to make use of Pinewood's Atlanta-based studio.

When *Star Wars* came to Pinewood, it brought with it some new villains of the First Order, including Kylo Ren (Adam Driver), seen here in 2015's *Star Wars Episode VII: The Force Awakens*.

The production of *Les Misérables*
(2012) required the height of
what was at the time Pinewood's
newest – and highest – stage
to create its French city under
siege. As Pinewood adds new
stages, they continue to build up
to accommodate the demands of
bigger – and taller – movies.

Disney brought their recent series of live-action remakes and reimaginings of their animated classics to the studios, locating such massive global hits as *Maleficent*, Branagh's *Cinderella* and *Beauty and the Beast* at the studios, re-establishing a relationship that Walt Disney himself had originally forged with J. Arthur Rank and his studio back in the early 1950s.

And once Disney acquired a little company by the name of Lucasfilm for a not so inconsiderable $4 billion – there was really only one place to go.

'I think that every single set on *Episode VII,* every single prop and costume that we started to create had this kind of historical relevance to *Star Wars*, and it became something that everyone got excited about.'

Producer Kathleen Kennedy on bringing a new *Star Wars* film to Pinewood

Producer Kathleen Kennedy was all too aware of the significance of bringing a production of the scale and calibre of a new *Star Wars* movie to a studio.

'I think that every single set on *Episode VII*, every single prop and costume that we started to create had this kind of historical relevance to *Star Wars*, and it became something that everyone got excited about. And certainly shooting on the *Millennium Falcon* was a perfect example because the minute everybody sets foot on that set, the minute Harrison Ford set foot on that set, it was akin to a religious experience!'

Star Wars: The Force Awakens shot at Pinewood throughout 2015, under a heavily maintained veil of secrecy, and when the film opened in December of that year it became one of the highest-grossing films of all time. It cemented a relationship between Pinewood and Lucasfilm, with both the first *Star Wars* standalone movie *Rogue One: A Star Wars Story*, and finally *Episode VIII* moving on to the lot the following year.

'We have pretty much taken over the whole studio,' laughs Kennedy. 'I think that we will continue to shoot on at least eight to ten stages per movie. So where we've got an overlap – like with *Rogue One* going into *Episode VIII* – we are building one film while prepping the other, and eventually the two shall meet. We have a lot of changeovers we had to do. On *Episode VIII*, we had close to 125 sets.'

But lest anyone think that Pinewood has solely become the home of the blockbuster, the studio firmly remains an equal-opportunities studio, playing host to such low - budget success stories as the Oscar-winning *Ex Machina*.

Despite often playing host to some of the biggest movies in cinema history, Pinewood still finds a way to accommodate some of the smaller, more visionary pieces that in their own way help redefine the art of film. Here, writer turned first-time director Alex Garland guides Alicia Vikander to global stardom as the AI Ava in *Ex Machina*, filmed largely on the stages of Pinewood in 2015.

When James Bond moves out, Meryl Streep and friends move in, and turn the 007 Stage into a Greek island for huge international hit musical *Mamma Mia* (2008).

Meryl Streep would win her third Oscar for bringing former British Prime Minister Margaret Thatcher back to life in *The Iron Lady* in 2011 at Pinewood.

RIGHT: Powerful in front of the camera; looking equally powerful behind it – Angelina Jolie's *Maleficent* helped usher in the new era of Disney live-action reworkings of their classic animated canon at Pinewood in 2014, something that continues at the studio to this day and beyond.

'I think it's a perception of the industry that there's no room for smaller films but we've got quite a good record in that area,' sales director – film Noel Tovey says. 'Something like *Ex Machina* for DNA was shot here at Pinewood. Something like *Les Misérables*, which seemed like a bigger film, but it was just two stages here and exteriors. In the scheme of things, it was quite a small film set. The scale of the movie looked great because they had the Richard Attenborough Stage where they built a three-storey set.'

So, as Pinewood Studios marks its eightieth year, it is not only a global brand, but probably the biggest and most well-known film studio in the world.

But where did it all begin?

Kenneth Branagh has been coming back to both Pinewood and Shepperton for most of his film-making career. He returned in 2015 to film Disney's *Cinderella* and its fairytale sets in and around Pinewood.

WHERE IT ALL BEGAN

J. ARTHUR RANK wanted to make religious movies. He was, after all, a devout man, who had been raised in the Methodist Church. He saw the medium of film as a way of promoting his faith. From such humble beginnings he rose to become Britain's biggest ever movie mogul, his legacy being one of the greatest film factories the world has ever known.

Joseph Arthur Rank was born on 23 December 1888 in Kingston upon Hull. His father, Joseph Rank, ran a flour-milling business that had already been in the family for generations and would make both men millionaires. Discouraged in his academic studies by his father, who assured him that his destiny was to follow him into the family firm, Arthur attempted to strike out on his own by forming a separate company, Peterkins Self-Raising Flour. When this failed, he went to work for, and with, his father (eventually inheriting the company upon his father's death in 1943).

Arthur was well into his forties before he had anything to do with the world of film. In the late 1920s, Arthur began to teach at Sunday school. It was here that he hit upon the idea of showing religious-themed films to the congregation. In his mind it was a means of bringing people to God, and it was an idea that proved a success. Soon he was renting projection equipment and showing these films to other churches up and down the country. But whilst he was impressed by the impact of his actions, he was less than satisfied with the quality of the films he was screening.

'I saw that religious films could be a great power for good,' he later recalled. 'I also saw it was no use giving people in churches cheap, badly made films when they could see up-to-date, well-made films at cinemas during the week. I saw that the thing to do was to have a hand in their making myself.'

In 1934, with this purpose in mind, he formed the Religious Film Society (affiliated with the religious propaganda group the Guilds of Light). Their first production was *The Mastery of Christ* (later retitled *Mastership*), a twenty-minute short that was first screened in April 1934. It cost the company £2,700 to produce.

As J. Arthur continued buying projectors for Methodist churches and self-distributing his own film and others, he struck a deal with one of the largest production–distribution companies in the country, Gaumont-British, to produce three more of his own religious-themed movies.

Rank's beginnings in the film business were admittedly small. But in just over a year, he had parlayed screening films at his local church into a distribution company

Rank confers with director Carol Reed, whose *Talk of the Devil* would become the first film to be fully produced at the newly opened Pinewood Studios in 1936.

PRECEDING PAGE: Studio founder and studio builder, J. Arthur Rank.

Heatherden Hall and its ornamental gardens – the beginnings of Pinewood.

of his own, and made the leap into film production. He saw the impact film had on his own, admittedly limited, audience, and was keenly aware that this could be built upon. But first he would need to learn more about the world of cinema.

At this time in England there were a number of small film studios in active operation, churning out product for ever-hungry audiences. From Elstree to Wembley to Borehamwood to Shepherd's Bush, Hammersmith to Teddington, Denham to Shepperton, film production was rife. But these studios and others were fairly small in scale, and certainly small in the nature of their productions, which constantly fought for attention against the bigger, glossier, altogether more glamorous movies that were flooding in from America.

What the UK needed was a production facility to rival that of Hollywood. This was an idea that had already been sown in the mind of Sir Auckland Geddes when he first visited Hollywood shortly after World War I. Geddes, an academic, politician and, later, diplomat, saw what he termed the 'close-to-the-job life' behind the success of the studios there and believed it was something that could be duplicated back home in the UK.

Geddes joined forces with Charles Boot, head of the Henry Boot and Sons building company, and together they set to work designing a large-scale Hollywood-style film studio, initially to be based at Elstree. Plans were drawn up but shelved and Geddes decided to abandon the project, feeling that it was simply not the right time to go ahead with such a sizeable venture. Boot, however, remained determined to fulfil his dream of a Hollywood-like studio and working community combined. For the next decade he searched for a place to base his project, and in 1934 he bought Heatherden Hall.

'Heatherden Hall was a mansion with the stateliness of a dowager, but Colonel Morden treated it like a mistress, spending – lavishing – thousands of pounds on it.'

Located seventeen miles west of central London in Iver Heath, Buckinghamshire, Heatherden Hall was a grand mansion built in the early nineteenth century. Under the ownership of Dr Drury Levin, it had been the site of many noted garden parties and lavish social gatherings.

The building really came into its own, however, when it was purchased by Canadian financier (and later Member of Parliament for Chiswick and Brentford) Lieutenant Colonel Grant Morden, who spent what was said to be in the region of £300,000 upgrading the property, adding an indoor swimming pool, a squash court and a Turkish bath alongside marble bathrooms, a ballroom, billiard room, tennis courts and over sixteen acres of beautiful ornamental gardens. It was said of his newly refurbished home, 'Heatherden Hall was a mansion with the stateliness of a dowager, but Colonel Morden treated it like a mistress, spending – lavishing – thousands of pounds on it.'

As Morden's life in British politics expanded, so did the function of his house, which became something of a meeting place for political figures. Indeed, in 1921 the Anglo-Irish Treaty was signed there. Morden himself, however, lost most of his wealth in the financial collapse of the early 1930s, eventually dying bankrupt in 1934. On 25 September of that year, Heatherden Hall went up for auction. Estate agents Goddard and Smith, handling the sale, described the house as a 'luxuriously appointed, imposing Georgian mansion (upon which vast sums have been spent from time to time) with its very valuable furniture and contents'. Its decor was 'tasteful and costly throughout', and in addition to mains electric light, it boasted its own water source, central heating and telephone (just the one, it appears).

An image from the 1934 Heatherden Hall auction document. Describing the 'elegant drawing room' as 'about 31-ft by 17-ft' with 'handsomely carved white marble mantlepiece' and 'ceiling in relief and centre arch with fluted column supports each end, after the Grinling Gibbons style, heating by radiators'.

FOLLOWING PAGE: Pinewood – the studio that came to life behind Heatherden Hall, seen from the air, in 1936, the year of its opening – and in more recent times, in 2016.

The property could be reached by three driveways, each with its own lodge entrance: in addition there were garages, stables (with two flats above), dog kennels, a bailiff's house, four bungalows and cottages, plus 158 acres of land, which included tennis courts (both clay and grass), a walled kitchen garden, ornamental gardens and woodland.

Charles Boot bought the whole thing for £35,000.

Over the years, Boot had kept his dream of a studio complex alive, and now in Heatherden Hall he believed he had found the perfect place to bring his vision to life. However, whilst he could afford to buy the property, he couldn't necessarily afford to build his studio.

J. Arthur Rank, meanwhile, was continuing with his expansion into the movie business.

'The view across the fields on the approach road to Pinewood was broken only by a cluster of tall pine trees, and then as if from nowhere appeared a mock Tudor double-lodge entrance, and a friendly commissionaire. It was just like arriving at a stately home.'
Sir Roger Moore

John Corfield had studied law at Liverpool University before fighting in World War I. After the war, he had made a low-budget film and been hired by the army to take films and projectors all over the world to entertain the troops abroad. On one such trip, to Bermuda, he met Lady Yule of Bricket Wood, the recently widowed (and extremely wealthy) wife of jute magnate Sir David Yule. Lady Yule seemed determined to enjoy her inheritance, travelling the world, big-game hunting and the like. Corfield invited her to see one of his films and Lady Yule was not impressed.

'What can you expect for eight thousand pounds a picture?' he said.

'It's absurd to let money stand in the way,' Lady Yule replied. 'Let's see if we can't do any better.'

Back in England, Corfield set about looking for further financial backing for a proposed new company. One of his colleagues, Graham Glegg, a prominent Methodist, arranged a meeting with Rank to discuss a potential partnership deal. When Glegg was unable to make the meeting himself, Corfield stepped in. Rank showed Corfield his *Mastership*, and Corfield agreed to produce two new religious-themed films for him at a cost of £4,500.

But soon Corfield was talking to Rank about his partnership with Lady Yule, and their plans to make a feature film of John Bunyan's *The Pilgrim's Progress*. Rank was interested in the project, and a meeting was set up with Lady Yule, during which the three of them agreed to form British National Films.

Corfield had approached Rank not for his burgeoning interest and involvement in cinema, but simply for his money. (Lady Yule seemed to be more focused on the fun and adventure of it.) The fact that both men worked together on Rank's religious films helped their relationship, but was by no means the motivating factor for their partnership. They were businessmen first and foremost and saw cinema as a great opportunity for success.

Although their plans for *The Pilgrim's Progress* were eventually abandoned, British National Films shot their first production in 1935. *Turn of the Tide*, adapted from

Parliamentary Secretary to the Board of Trade, Dr Leslie Burgin had the honour of performing the official opening ceremony for the new Pinewood Studios on 30 September 1936 – seen here flanked by Carol Reed, producer Jack Raymond, and actors Sally Ellers and Ricardo Cortez.

RIGHT: It's for you! Prop master Bert Guitens (standing) and assistant pick up a call from Pinewood's varied collection of telephone props, 1938.

the 1932 book *Three Fevers* by Leo Walmsley, was directed by Norman Walker and starred Wilfrid Lawson and Geraldine Fitzgerald (who went on to work with Orson Welles' Mercury Theatre before establishing a long and successful career in Hollywood).

The film was shot at Elstree, which to Rank's mind provided far from perfect conditions. Thinking with his mill-owning, factory-assembly-line hat on, he couldn't help but notice the waste incurred by working in such a small studio environment. Both money and time were lost when only a single stage was being used; production would literally grind to a halt as one set was struck and another one built. He discussed the issue with Corfield.

'Most studios in this country are obsolete,' he observed.

'Why don't we build one?' Corfield replied.

Charles Boot, meanwhile, was busy remodelling Heatherden Hall as a luxury country club. After all, the sales particulars had noted that it was 'suitable for hotel, institution or clinic'. He was going with something akin to the former, and had

converted the ballroom into a 150-seat restaurant that opened out to the gardens, whilst the bedrooms had been refitted as luxury suites. Boot spent eleven months rebuilding his property, and when it was ready to open, he had a brochure printed declaring that it offered 'all the luxury of a first-class hotel combined with the charm and informal atmosphere of a country manor. Utter contentment, induced by the peace of its country setting and the keen stimulation of the club's indoor and outdoor attractions, will be the lot of all who enter.' (He even went as far as to install a fruit machine in the bar!)

'I named it Pinewood because of the number of those trees which grow there, and because it seemed to suggest something of the American film centre in its second syllable.'

Charles Boot on naming Pinewood

However, he had by no means abandoned his plans to build a major film studio. To this aim he had also purchased some land opposite Heatherden Hall, still determined to realise his notion of a close-to-the job living environment.

It was with this plan still firmly in his mind that Boot chose at this time to call his new estate Pinewood, explaining in later life that he named it so 'because of the number of those trees which grow there, and because it seemed to suggest something of the American film centre in its second syllable'.

With his country club now up and running, he decamped to Hollywood to view for himself the designs and workings of the major Hollywood studios, and by November of 1934 he and his team of architects had begun work on Pinewood, the studio. However, he quickly realised that financially he was not in a position to bring his long-held dream to life.

Boot was aware of Rank and his recent developments with British National Films. More importantly, he knew that both Rank and Yule represented money. So in December 1935 he met with Rank and told him of his plans for a large studio complex, complete with his (originally Geddes's) notion of a workforce that lived close to the job. The idea – and the opportunity – instantly appealed to Arthur, who had been disappointed with the inefficacy of filming at Elstree. He saw in the scope and scale of Pinewood an opportunity to use his flour-milling empire as a paradigm for film production.

The deal was quickly struck, and Pinewood Studios Limited was formed. The board of directors comprised Boot, Rank, Corfield and Corfield's son-in-law Spencer Reis.

What's a New Year's party without champagne? These oversized examples, however, were being stored away for another day at Pinewood, 4 January 1938.

'The person really responsible for the building of these studios is the late Mr Charles Boot. He had already bought the estate and had been to Hollywood and was very much wrapped up in the building of these studios.'

J. Arthur Rank pays tribute to Charles Boot

Always content to take a back seat when it came to business, Lady Yule asked Corfield to manage her interests.

At Pinewood's twenty-first-anniversary celebration, Rank paid tribute to Charles Boot, who had passed away in 1945.

'The person really responsible for the building of these studios is the late Mr Charles Boot. He, at the opening of this studio, said that if it had not been for me, the project would have fallen down, but he made a mistake. He was responsible for it, because I am quite sure that he would have found some other optimist to find the money. He had already bought the estate and had been to Hollywood and was very much wrapped up in the building of these studios.'

In early 1936, a fire tore through Elstree Studios, owned by the British and Dominions Film Corporation. With money from the insurance, and a need for new facilities, British and Dominions merged with Pinewood in February of that year, offering both new investment capital and production commitments. It also brought several new players into the fold and on to the board. Amongst those new faces was Richard Norton, who became the first managing director of Pinewood Studios.

Norton had begun his career in high finance before working for the UK offices of, first, Paramount Pictures, and then United Artists. Amongst his many achievements during this period was to bring the producer Alexander Korda to England, where he made *The Private Life of Henry VIII*, starring Charles Laughton, which became a major worldwide success in 1934. Korda himself, meanwhile, would eventually take charge of Shepperton Studios and become the only movie mogul in the UK to rival J. Arthur Rank.

As construction continued apace in the spring of 1936, John Corfield took a leaf out of Boot's book and went to explore studio design in other countries, in this case the cavernous sound stages of Germany. However, it was Pinewood's first general manager, James Sloan, who would be credited with the majority of the studio's design. He oversaw the operation from November 1935 to completion in September 1936, a task that involved more than 1,500 workmen, employed through forty-six

Entrance to South Corridor, the original part of the studio built in 1936. It adjoins A, B, C and D stage to A-G Blocks, allowing cast and crew to get their hair, make-up and wardrobe done in blocks and hop across the corridor onto set. Commonly used as a filming location such as a hospital corridor in *Carry On Matron*.

separate contractors, along with 2,300 tons of steel, 20,000 cubic yards of concrete, 300,000 yards of soundproofing materials, 15,000 yards of asphalt and some six million bricks. In addition, over sixty miles of electrical cables were used. The total cost of construction was a little north of £1,000,000.

'Compared with the majestic pine, the holly is a bush or stunted tree.'

Dr Leslie Burgin makes a sly reference to Pinewood's US competitors, opening day, 1936

The stages at Pinewood slowly come to life, early 1936. The first brick was laid in December 1935 and a new stage was completed every three weeks. Six million bricks and nine months later the cameras were ready to turn. 1,500 men were employed during construction and the cost of building the studio ran to over £1 million.

Pinewood offered what was termed the unit system – two stages, one large (measuring 165 by 110 feet), one small (110 by 82 feet), grouped together as one unit. Around these were built offices, dressing rooms, make-up rooms, a camera room, a monitor room and a self-sufficient ventilating plant. The walls of the stages were made of one-foot-thick solid concrete, and large electrically operated doors ensured complete soundproofing. Each stage also contained a large water tank that could hold up to 65,000 gallons and could be heated if so desired. An overhead electrical system was in place on each stage to keep the studio floor free of electrical cables (Pinewood being the first studio in Europe to employ such a system). The dressing rooms ranged from those for star players to spaces that could house up to 1,500 extras at a time.

The various workshops on site offered the skills of carpenters, plasterers, painters, modellers, blacksmiths and tinsmiths, and there were also camera repair shops and lamp and timber stores. Twenty-five editing rooms were available, and a three-storey sound building contained two screening theatres, each capable of housing a full symphony orchestra.

There were eight such units planned for Pinewood, to be constructed around a central area designed to house workshops, sound, art, props and wardrobe, all of which would be equidistant from each of the stage units. This would allow numerous productions to film at once and make use of the facilities the studio provided as a whole. It was described as an architectural equation – distance equals time equals money – and at the time, it made Pinewood amongst the most modern studios in the world.

Naturally enough, Pinewood also had its own powerhouse, capable of generating 2,300 kilowatts, its own water supply and, in light of the recent fire at Elstree, twenty hydrants and 1,000 sprinklers, which were capable of flooding any stage to a depth of nine feet within three minutes.

And if that wasn't enough, there were forty-eight acres of backlot, along with a further sixteen acres of Colonel Morden's ornamental gardens (all electrically wired for exterior filming), for any incoming production to turn into anything or anywhere their hearts desired.

The Chairman and Directors
of
PINEWOOD   STUDIOS   LIMITED
cordially invite

W. Gerhold, Esq

to the

LUNCHEON & OFFICIAL OPENING OF THE STUDIOS
on

WEDNESDAY, 30th SEPTEMBER, 1936

R.S.V.P. *Pinewood Studios*
Iver Heath, Bucks.

12-30 for 1 p.m.

The hottest ticket just outside of
town! An invitation to Pinewood's
opening day ceremony,
30 September 1936.

Pinewood Studios was officially opened on 30 September 1936. The large and lavish ceremony took place on D Stage, with over a thousand guests. Dr Leslie Burgin, the Parliamentary Secretary to the Board of Trade, did the honours, and in his speech made a sly dig at the studio's competitors across the water. 'Compared with the majestic pine, the holly is a bush or stunted tree,' he said. 'May the quality of what you produce break down all the doors that at present bar the way to British films.'

Charles Boot's Pinewood country club still continued to function, although an administration building for the studio was built behind it that included, amongst other things, a restaurant capable of catering to five hundred diners. It was anticipated that the business of the club would combine with that of the studio, with one publication saying at the time of the studio's opening, 'It should appeal particularly to those concerned in film production for their especial needs will be anticipated and appropriately catered for by its expert service and the management's special attention to studio conditions and demands.'

The *Cinema News and Property Gazette* published a special edition to coincide with the launch. Within its pages, Pinewood board member Herbert Wilcox took time to express his feelings about the opening of this new studio, referring to the facility as a well-oiled machine, and mentioning his intention to coax Hollywood talent to these new and superior facilities. He also discussed his philosophy of film production in general, emphasising his preference for independent production over the Hollywood studio system.

'The new Pinewood Studios are already becoming established amongst the foremost studios in world film production … To Iver also I plan to bring famous artistes from Hollywood and abroad. These will no longer be asked to submit to "scratch" conditions as in the past, but will find the Pinewood Studios equal and in many ways superior to any they have worked in. They will have the best possible chance to give the best possible performance.

'But there is another and all-important reason why I am proud to work at Iver. Pinewood Studios are the perfect workshop for the independent producer. The organisation and resources there put him on an equal footing with the mightiest producing companies.

'More and more it becomes my conviction that the future of the industry lies in this individualism rather than in collectivism or the mass production of films. At Iver he will have the finest opportunity of fulfilling that destiny.'

Richard Norton also wrote a piece for the launch-day magazine supplement, his entitled 'What Pinewood Offers'. Here he discussed how Pinewood would bring the glamour of Hollywood to the Home Counties and highlighted the intention of the studio to create a film-making community.

Dr Leslie Burgin joins Sally Ellers, Carol Reed (leaning on the camera) and actor Robert Douglas, on the day of Pinewood's opening, 1936.

FOLLOWING PAGE: Pinewood goes live on television for the first time in September 1937, a year after its opening. Carry that cable, boys.

'British production has for years been sadly behind Hollywood in one important quality – glamour.

'Although in ability and enthusiasm the British studio worker is second to none in the world, he has so far lacked that extra impetus which living in a film community bestows. A deliberate and sincere attempt to remove this disadvantage has been made in the establishment of Pinewood as a residential studio group, with a club, and other social amenities. Workers will in no sense be "marooned" there; its proximity to London ensures that; the provision of communal facilities will afford opportunities for the "shop-talk" that has made the Hollywood studio worker a white-hot enthusiast.'

'It is no exaggeration to say that Pinewood is as great an improvement on the traditional British studio as the modern home is on the Victorian forerunner, proving that efficiency, economy and hygiene can be secured without loss of comfort.'

From an article by Richard Norton, opening day, 1936

Whilst this was not quite the idyllic close-to-the-job life as envisioned first by Geddes and later by Boot, who had purchased land adjacent to the studio for the potential housing of staff, it did still propose an ideology that set Pinewood apart from other studios.

Norton went on in his piece to discuss the recent disastrous fire at Elstree Studios, something that would, ironically, bring Pinewood its first production.

'It cannot be denied that the destruction by fire of the Elstree Studios at the beginning of the year was a serious blow to British and Dominions and the company's associated tenants; but good has certainly come out of evil in this case, in the acquisition of a substantial interest in Pinewood Studios.

'A new and attractive policy is being pursued inasmuch as tenant producers will have full access to every advantage Pinewood has to offer.'

Anna Neagle and Robert Douglas starred in *London Melody* (1937), a film that had started filming at Elstree Studios but completed its shoot at Pinewood, following a major fire at Elstree.

Norton's article also afforded him the opportunity to sing the praises of the talented team of technicians the studio had assembled as it opened its doors to the world.

'It has not hitherto been customary, for an example, for a space-renting company to offer, free of charge, the advice and co-operation of its expert technicians and

heads of department. This we do unreservedly, confident in the knowledge that our departmental heads form a team of experts unsurpassed in the country, whose co-operation must react favourably on the standard of production at Pinewood and thus greatly increase the studio's prestige.

'It will be readily appreciated that it is of the utmost importance to us that product bearing the mark "Made at Pinewood" shall be of the highest quality. Therefore it is not in pure benevolence that we offer these unique advantages, but in a far-sighted policy of self-interest.'

Going on to describe the state-of-the-art quality of his new studio's equipment and the fact that it offered 'electric power sufficient to supply the needs of a city', Norton concluded by highlighting the financial advantages of the studio, designed to work as smoothly and efficiently as one of Rank's flour mills.

'By careful planning, wastage of money, time and temper have been brought to an incredible minimum, and the old bogey of breakdown, costing thousands in cash, and still more in nervous strain, has been laid at last.

'In fact, it is no exaggeration to say that Pinewood is as great an improvement on the traditional British studio as the modern home is on the Victorian forerunner, proving that efficiency, economy and hygiene can be secured without loss of comfort.'

Norton's article was little short of a manifesto for the new studio, and a gauntlet thrown down to Hollywood.

Herbert Wilcox would become the first film-maker to shoot at Pinewood, finishing off *London Melody*, a British and Dominions production that had been started at Elstree but was interrupted by the fire.

Before he picked up the megaphone, however, Wilcox announced on Pinewood's launch day a £1 million programme of four new films about to start production at the studio, all to be distributed by United Artists. The first of these would be Carol Reed's *A Man with Your Voice*, which became the first film to be fully produced at the new Pinewood Studios.

Carol Reed made many of his early movies at Pinewood. Here he consults his notes and crew on the set of *The Fallen Idol* (1948).

London Melody (1937) aimed to bring the glamour of Hollywood to Pinewood Studios, Iver Heath.

SHEPPERTON
FLICKERS INTO FRAME

H AVING ESTABLISHED HIMSELF as the proprietor of a successful camera rental business, Norman Loudon discovered a market for flicker books, small novelty books in which a sense of motion was created by flicking the pages, each of which featured a sequential photo of an event, thus creating the impression of a moving image. After making a considerable amount of money with such items, Loudon decided that the next move was film itself. To aid his plans, in 1929 he bought the Littleton Park Estate, with the express purpose of converting it into a film studio.

The grand house came with sixty-five acres of land, and Loudon acquired a further seventy acres that included an area of the local woods and part of the River Ash. The whole thing cost the fledgling entrepreneur around £5,000. In 1930, he registered Flicker Film Productions and began converting his estate into sound studios, which opened for business in 1932.

Littleton Park, which would eventually become the home of Shepperton Studios, lies nineteen miles south of Pinewood Studios, and twelve miles outside London, in the heart of the Middlesex countryside. The estate itself can be dated back to the seventh century, when it was run by Westminster monks. In 1689, a manor house was built on the site, from a design by noted architect Christopher Wren.

In 1901, the manor and its surrounding lands were bought by Richard Burbage. Burbage, who had made his fortune as a retailer in London, had risen, a decade before his purchase, to take over the management of Harrods, now London's most prestigious department store. The considerable wealth his position afforded him gave him the opportunity to buy his country home.

Burbage spent many years building up the house and the surrounding grounds, and would often hold lavish garden parties there for the staff of Harrods, as well as dinner parties for the store's buyers. Foreshadowing its later purpose, he also allowed films to be shot there, making use of the house's ballroom and conservatory as locations, much as Loudon would years later.

In 1917, Burbage – by now Sir Richard, having been awarded a baronetcy the previous year – died, and the property was bought by Commander Sir Edward Nicholl, a Member of Parliament and shipping magnate, who would later name a navy ship, the SS *Littleton*, after his country pile. (By an interesting coincidence,

as Commander Nicholl was buying Littleton Park, a few miles north, Lieutenant Colonel Grant Morden was busy adding a swimming pool and more to his recently purchased Heatherden Hall.) Twelve years later, Loudon bought the estate from Nicholl.

When the studio opened in 1932, it was kitted out with state-of-the-art equipment for the making of talkies (talking pictures), as reflected in its name – Sound City Film Producing and Recording Studios. Loudon financed the venture independently, his initial investment of £20,950 coming from himself and a mixture of wealthy private individuals. With two large sound stages, in its first year of operation Sound City was home to the production of two features and five short films. The first feature was *Watch Beverley*, produced by New Zealand-born Ivor Campbell (under Loudon's close eye). Having migrated into film from the stock exchange, Campbell turned director for the studio's second offering, *Reunion*, and would helm another twenty pictures for Loudon before losing his life in World War II. Wanting to surround himself with a core group of reliable talent, Loudon would also re-employ *Watch Beverley*'s director, Arthur Maude, for another two movies the following year.

The initial output at Sound City was varied, from melodrama to comedies, even stretching to a musical, *Talking Feet* in 1937.

The Old Hall at the Littleton Park Estate, which was converted to house Sound City Film Producing and Recording Studios, later to become Shepperton Studios.

PRECEDING PAGE: Pinewood's initial competitor – then known as Sound City – as seen from above.

By 1934, David Lean, who would go on to make many pictures at Shepperton, was working at the studios as an editor, on that year's *Song of the Plough*. As he explained in later years, Lean found his early work inspiring, despite what he saw as its lack of quality. 'I worked on a lot of bad pictures, and bad pictures are very good for one's ego, because the worse they are the more chance you have of making them better.'

The same year that Lean was toiling away learning how to improve other film-makers' bad pictures, often editing more than one at a time, Loudon produced a brochure to present the advantages of his studio to the world. This promotional booklet stated that Sound City 'proudly offers to the film industry the evidence of its unique advantages as a production centre', boasting that more than twenty-five productions had been made there in 1934 alone. An aerial photo of the studio adorned the cover, with the caption: 'In this aerial shot of Sound City, there are Five of 1935's biggest films in production at the same time – (1) Gaumont-British filming *The Iron Duke* on the Sound City lawns; (2) London Films making *Sanders*, with three hundred natives encamped in the huge African Village on the unique Sound City River; (3) Will Fyffe working on the country village set in *Rolling Home*, a Sound City picture; (4) Tom Walls directing the Gaumont-British picture *Lady in Danger*; and (5) In Number 2 Sound Stage Wainwright's production *Emil and the Detectives*.'

Welcome – Shepperton Studios is open for business.

LEFT: Alexander Korda used the grounds and surrounding area of Sound City Studios to recreate an African village for *Sanders of the River*, directed by his brother Zoltan in 1935.

The brochure went on to enthuse how 'the Studio "Lot" of over 70 acres of unrivalled exteriors has everything the Film Producer wants, from Bond Street to the Jungle'. Having detailed the varied state-of-the-art equipment available for all aspects of production and post-production, and the imminent construction of two additional sound stages, Loudon's booklet was eager to point out the money-saving opportunities Sound City had to offer.

'The Studio "Lot" of over 70 acres of unrivalled exteriors has everything the Film Producer wants, from Bond Street to the Jungle.'

Norman Loudon's brochure presents the advantages of Sound City to the world

'An enormous stock of existing sets affords the Producer every opportunity for saving money: permanent Street Sets and Country Villages are already built on the "Lot"; there is more than three quarters of a mile of river, and a concrete pool 17,000 square feet for exterior and trick work. Magnificent offices and living accommodation in the Mansion for artistes and production staff.'

Last, but not least, it was easy to get to. 'The newest of London's arterial roads, the "Chertsey Road", will practically pass the gates of Sound City from Hammersmith. Electric trains from Waterloo or Earl's Court to Shepperton Station. Studios 5 minutes from station.'

Loudon had always planned Sound City to attract production companies to its facilities, many of whom became resident on the lot. The variety of locations this backlot afforded led to a number of productions wanting to shoot there. Gaumont-British moved its production of *The Wandering Jew*, starring Conrad Veidt and Peggy Ashcroft, across from Twickenham to take advantage of Sound City's woodland exteriors. Basil Dean's production of Jerome K. Jerome's *Three Men in a Boat* made use of the River Ash (or 'the unique Sound City River' as the brochure had called it), whilst the historical drama *Drake of England* went as far as recreating Tilbury Docks on the studio's stretch of the River Ash.

Production was booming, encouraging Loudon to plough as much as £60,000 into another historical piece, *Colonel Blood* in 1934.

This latter move was in some part an attempt to compete with another film-maker who would have a huge impact on the growth and development of Shepperton Studios, and the British film industry in general. In 1934, Alexander Korda's lavish large-scale production of *The Private Life of Henry VIII* became a massive global success, and one of the highest-grossing British pictures to that date, earning a then world-record-breaking take of $18,400 in one day at New York's Radio City Music Hall.

Alexander Korda, the man who would come to own and run Shepperton Studios, poses with actress Merle Oberon and Hollywood mogul Sam Goldwyn in 1935.

Born in Hungary on 16 September 1893, Alexander Korda began his career in journalism, writing and publishing film magazines. This soon led to offers to write screenplays, his first being 1914's *Watchhouse in the Carpathians*. His poor eyesight excused him from military service in World War I; instead he went to work at Budapest's Pedagogical Studio, where he made his directing debut. Korda was arrested following the overthrow of the Hungarian Soviet Republic, due to his association with that government. Following his release, he left his native country, never to return.

Disillusioned by what he saw as the restrictive nature of the studio system in Hollywood, Alexander Korda decided to return to Europe, settling in Britain in 1932.

The film producer's career continued apace over the next few years, after he relocated to Vienna, where he found great success with his 1920 production of *The Prince and the Pauper*. A large-scale take on the story of Samson and Delilah was less successful, however, and Korda moved on to work in Berlin. In 1919, he married the Hungarian actress Maria Corda, who rose to become a successful screen actress in Germany, often working in tandem with her husband. In December 1926, First National Pictures offered them a joint contract, and the couple relocated to America.

Korda's first American film was *The Stolen Bride* in 1927; its casting of Billie Dove over his wife was to foreshadow the troubles their marriage was about to face, something that was exacerbated by the arrival thereafter of talking pictures. Korda himself found it easy to adapt to this new form, which rapidly exploded first in Hollywood and then throughout the world after the release of Al Jolson's *The Jazz Singer*. Maria Corda, however, always a success in the era of silent pictures, retained too strong an accent to find success in the talkies, and the strain of her husband's rising success and her own diminishing star power led the couple to divorce in 1930.

Disillusioned by what he saw as the restrictive nature of the studio system in Hollywood, coupled with his financial losses in the Wall Street Crash of 1929, Korda decided to return to Europe, settling in Britain in 1932.

Here he established a new production company, London Films (using Big Ben as its on-screen logo), and recruited his younger brothers, Zoltan and Vincent, also in exile from Hungary, to work with him, as director and art director respectively. Now in a position to make the kind of movies he had always planned to, Korda directed and produced *The Private Life of Henry VIII*, which not only became a massive box

office success but was nominated for two Academy Awards, including Best Picture, winning the Best Actor Oscar for its leading man, Charles Laughton.

In 1935, London Films bought Hills House in Buckinghamshire and opened Denham Film Studios (a company that would later merge with Pinewood). But the year before that, Korda, as producer, found himself in need of a river on which to build an African village for the adventure *Sanders of the River*, directed by his brother Zoltan.

This led him for the first time to Shepperton, a studio he would later come to run.

Korda studies his shot on the set of *The Private Life of Henry VIII* (1933).

Charles Laughton and co-star Merle Oberon stroll around whilst filming Alexander Korda's hugely successful *The Private Life of Henry VIII* (1933).

ALL THIS,
AND WORLD WAR II

W ITHIN FOUR WEEKS of opening its doors, Pinewood Studios had four films in production (with distribution already secured). Within three months, eight films were up and running in Iver Heath.

Both Pinewood and Sound City at Shepperton remained buoyant in their early years, thanks in part to what became known as the 'quota quickies'. With the British public's ravenous appetite for cinema ever growing, it was noted by the government that much of the revenue from this most lucrative of pastimes was leaving the country and returning to Hollywood. Thus in 1927, the Cinematograph Films Act was passed, which decreed that Britain must produce and distribute a certain number of films per year, ensuring income for the country and employment throughout the industry. For the next ten years, British cinemas were required to show a quota of home-made films. These movies were often made quickly (hence the name) and only ran around the sixty-minute mark, with budgets in the region of £6,000 per production, and film stock valued at around £1 per foot. Music and effects were taken from stock recordings.

These films usually played as support features to a bigger (often Hollywood) production, and quite often weren't even viewed at all, with many members of the public choosing to show up for the main feature and ignoring the support altogether. Yet they helped keep the British film industry alive, and provided many, both in front of and behind the camera, with some of their earliest work in film, amongst them famed cinematographer Freddie Francis, writer Terence Rattigan, and actors such as Rex Harrison, Margaret Rutherford, Wendy Hiller, George Sanders and even Vivien Leigh (who in later life would often choose to ignore this early stage of her career).

The 1927 Act stipulated that what it considered a British film was one that was produced by a British-controlled company and written by a British citizen, with all studio scenes shot at a film studio located within the British Empire or Commonwealth, and at least 75 per cent of all salaries paid to British subjects (thus allowing for the inclusion of a major international film star if the production could afford it).

By 1935, the quota of British films being screened in UK cinemas was as high as 20 per cent, yet these were not the only productions being brought to life in these two new purpose-built studios.

Hungarian producer Gabriel Pascal persuaded J. Arthur Rank to back his production of an adaptation of George Bernard Shaw's *Pygmalion*. Shaw had so far avoided having his work brought to the screen, but this one, starring Wendy Hiller and Leslie Howard (who also co-directed with Anthony Asquith), was a

resounding success at the international box office and garnered four Academy Award nominations, including one for Best Picture. Looking back on its making in a 1966 television interview, the then Dame Wendy Hiller recalled the relative splendour of shooting at Pinewood at the time.

'I didn't know how lucky I was to be virtually living in a country house,' the actress recollected. 'The staff were very efficient and attentive and it was lovely to be able to walk through the gardens, beautifully planted and maintained, to make-up and get into my chair and have my hair set and have a white-coated waiter bring me my breakfast. That was film-making, or rather that was film-making at Pinewood.'

Meanwhile, J. Arthur Rank was busy consolidating his power at Pinewood by buying out Lady Yule's share of the business. Conversely, he sold her his shares in British National, which she then continued to run alongside John Corfield.

Wendy Hiller starred as Eliza Doolittle in 1938's *Pygmalion*, one of the last films to be completed at Pinewood before the studio found itself closed for the duration of World War II.

PRECEDING PAGE: Closed down – but still shooting. The Army Film and Photographic Unit found itself housed at a temporarily requisitioned Pinewood for the duration of World War II.

At the same time, Rank teamed up with C. M. Woolf to rescue Gaumont-British, giving him a controlling interest in the most powerful distributors in the country, something that was consolidated further when Rank invested in the Odeon chain, run by Hungarian émigré Oscar Deutsch, who needed investment capital to fund his attempt to crack the American market.

'It was lovely to be able to walk through the gardens to make-up and get into my chair and have my hair set and have a white-coated waiter bring me my breakfast. That was film-making, or rather that was film-making at Pinewood.'

Dame Wendy Hiller

During this active period, a young Alfred Hitchcock completed *Young and Innocent*, his first film at Pinewood. Bound for Hollywood, Hitchcock would not return to the studios again until his penultimate film, *Frenzy*, brought him back to the UK in 1971.

The Cinematograph Films Act was modified in 1938 (it would remain in existence in some form until it was repealed by the Films Act of 1960), and these changes led to the death of the quota quickie, which caused an overall downturn in production in the UK. Whilst British movies would still be made, the idea was to make fewer, but bigger and better films. A noble concept, but one that would have a significant impact on British studios. In an attempt to counteract this, Pinebrook Films was formed (spearheaded by the studio's managing director, Richard Norton) specifically to produce low-budget movies.

Over at Denham Studios, meanwhile, Alexander Korda's London Films was experiencing financial difficulties of its own, as Korda's increasingly large-budget movies – *Things to Come*, *The Four Feathers*, *Elephant Boy* – failed to match his earlier success and make back their money at the box office. Rank saw an opportunity to strike and moved in to cover London's £1 million of debts with its backers, the Prudential Building Society (he would eventually buy out all of the Prudential's interests in the studio). In 1938, as a result of this, Denham was combined with Pinewood to form D&P Studios Ltd, an event that brought two of British cinema's leading players into each other's orbit for the first time, even if it did take the form of Rank buying out Korda's shares to facilitate the merger. Korda was so despondent over losing his share of Denham, and his recent movies failing to find success at the box office, that he would shortly move back to America, completing his film *The Thief of Baghdad* there, even though it had begun production in the UK.

Hitchcock pictured in the Pinewood gardens on 22 July 1971, whilst filming *Frenzy*.

Alfred Hitchcock makes his customary cameo appearance in *Young and Innocent* (1937), the first film he shot at Pinewood. And the last, until he returned for his penultimate picture, *Frenzy*, in 1972.

Despite the rapid expansion and amalgamation of his film interests, on Christmas Eve 1938 Rank closed the doors of Pinewood, due to a downturn in production, focusing the company's film-making at Denham Studios – which was currently home to Gabriel Pascal's production of another Shaw play, *Major Barbara*. An article in the *Daily Film Renter* stated that Pinewood was closing due to the 'fact that the existing state of British production is insufficient to warrant the current upkeep of equipment and personnel', with Richard Norton adding, 'In the immediate future, the facilities of Denham will be adequate for existing production schedules.'

However, activity at Denham, Shepperton and elsewhere was soon curtailed. On 3 September 1939, war was declared, and all British studios were closed down and requisitioned for government use. Film-makers from directors to actors to technicians of all manner went off to fight, and production in the UK for the most part ground to a halt for the duration.

Over the next six years, Pinewood would become home and haven to a number of government institutions, being used as a storage facility and seeing the creation of various armed forces film units. Shepperton, meanwhile, would make use of its remaining technicians, and the tradition of their work, manufacturing 'dummy' aeroplanes and tanks, whose deployment proved to be an invaluable decoy device throughout the war. (Denham remained open initially, as *Major Barbara* was running considerably over schedule – and budget.)

Initially, Pinewood was requisitioned by the army and used to store vital supplies such as sugar. Given the studio's proximity to, yet relative distance from, London (presumed to be a major bombing target), it was a perfect place to which to relocate many of the country's financial institutions. Thus, Lloyd's of London moved into the main house and its administration block the weekend before war was officially declared, its 500-plus staff for the most part accommodated nearby by canvassing local homes to take in these vital workers – surely not the original close-to-the-job life Sir Auckland Geddes and Charles Boot had once envisioned for the studio. The day after war was declared, Lloyd's opened for business as usual at their new Iver Heath address. The Royal Mint, meanwhile, took up residence on one of the studio's sound stages.

Pinewood got its own fire guard, largely comprised of ARP-trained Lloyd's employees. A lack of underground shelter led to instructions being issued for those on site to essentially run into the nearby woods if imminent attack was sounded.

As the war progressed, the largely female staff at Lloyd's were separated by a wire fence from the soldiers who arrived on site. These soldiers were largely there to man the film units that were stationed at Pinewood. Having realised the power of propaganda and film in wartime, and the need to use news images to convey the events of the war to those left behind at home, the government formed the Crown Film Unit in 1941, alongside the Army Film and Photography Unit (AFPU) and the

John Boulting (centre) directing his two young leads, Richard Attenborough (left) and Jack Watling, in *Aircrew* (1944), a production of the RAF Film Unit, which was based at Pinewood throughout the war years.

Royal Air Force Unit. All of them made their base at Pinewood – together with the Polish Air Force Film Unit. The studio's dressing rooms were used to house the men, many of whom had worked in the industry prior to the war and knew each other.

The all-important issue of the absence of the traditional mid-morning on-set tea break in such trying times was solved when a group of female volunteers from nearby town, Gerrards Cross, started bringing their mobile tea service to the studio for the men encamped there.

The men of these military film units were deployed all over the world to capture and relay the events of the war. Among those who went on to forge successful careers in the British film industry were future Shepperton Studio heads the Boulting Brothers.

Despite Pinewood's proximity to the capital, only one V-2 bomb found its way there during the war, exploding in a nearby field south of the studios.

The men of these military film units were deployed all over the world to capture and relay the events of the war. Needless to say, despite the circumstances, many of them benefited immensely from these experiences. Among those who went on to forge successful careers in the British film industry were future Shepperton Studio heads the Boulting Brothers, Roy and John (army and air force respectively), Hugh Stewart, who would go on to produce a dozen of Norman Wisdom's comedies and all three of Morecambe and Wise's big-screen outings, and a young soldier by the name of Richard Attenborough.

The units produced many significant and groundbreaking films during this period, including *Burma Victory*, *Malta GC*, *Left of the Line* and *Desert Victory*, Roy Boulting's documentary about Rommel's retreat, which marked Britain's first major victory in the war. The film won the young director an Academy Award in 1943. In stating the importance of the continued production of films during World War II, Michael Balcon (who remained head of Ealing Studios throughout the war) wrote in *Kinematograph Weekly*, 'The time will come during this war when a man behind a film camera will command the same respect as a man behind a gun.'

Although film production had ceased at Sound City over in Shepperton, the studio remained extremely active for the duration. Many of the technicians still available were employed to put their skills to the test, not by building props and sets for movies as they once had, but by constructing dummy aircraft and tanks. These facsimiles – essentially hollow wooden replicas of various military craft and weapons – were considered a vital component in the war effort, designed to confuse and distract the Luftwaffe over Britain, encouraging them to target what was essentially a field of wooden props rather than a factory of Hawker Hurricanes.

Many of the technicians still available were employed to put their skills to the test by constructing dummy aircraft and tanks – these facsimilies were considered a vital component of the war effort, designed to confuse and distract the Luftwaffe over Britain.

Shepperton continued with this kind of production throughout the war with these props being used in a similar decoying capacity all over the world. In addition, the studio gave over two of its sound stages to Tate & Lyle for the storage of sugar, which was now rationed, and when the nearby Vickers aircraft factory was bombed, production of Wellington bombers shifted to A and B Stages at Shepperton.

Many years after the event, it emerged that the studio was also used during this period as a place for the training of spies. Over in America, Alexander Korda too was playing his part in the war effort, and in the spying game. In the run-up to war breaking out, Korda had allowed his London Films European offices to be used by members of British intelligence. He opened up his West Coast office in the States for the same purpose. In 1941, he was rewarded for his covert war efforts with a knighthood, becoming the first film producer in Britain to be dubbed a 'Sir'.

The reality of life during wartime led more and more people to escape to the fantasies the movies had to offer, and cinema attendance was at an all-time high. Rank himself was determined not only to meet such demand, but to continue to build his business alongside it. In 1939, just as war was looming, he had purchased Amalgamated Studios at Elstree and swiftly leased it to the government as a records storage facility, for a tidy profit. In 1941, he paid three quarters of a million pounds to buy out the then troubled Gaumont-British distribution chain, and later that year, after the death of its founder Oscar Deutsch, he took full control of the Odeon chain. The death of C. M. Woolf in 1942 saw Rank assume full control of the Rank company and consolidate his rise from a miller who rented projectors to churches to the most powerful movie mogul the country had ever seen – all in under a decade.

In 1944, however, Rank's increasing dominance over the British film industry led to an investigation by the government. The ensuing Palache Report showed that whilst Rank was a prominent figure in the industry, his holdings – which comprised just under half of the studio space in the country and around 15 per cent of cinemas – did not constitute a monopoly, although it was determined that he should have

The True Glory (1945) – in part directed by Carol Reed – featured contributions from many of the military photographic units that had been stationed at Pinewood throughout the war. It won the Academy Award for Best Documentary Feature the following year.

to seek permission from the Board of Trade if he wished to open any additional cinemas.

That same year, Rank also visited Hollywood to see for himself how the system there worked and to find out what could be adapted for use back in his own studios. A Hollywood mogul of equal success but of a different stripe to Rank, David O. Selznick, was so taken by the Englishman that he set up a new production venture with him. Rank was so impressed by what he saw as he toured Universal Studios and its ilk that he would continue to send many of his own technicians and directors to Hollywood in the years to come to study and learn from American techniques in order to improve production back in the UK.

Rank's interests, however, were not always financial. Over at Denham Studios, which had continued production throughout the war, he helped establish Independent Producers Ltd, a unique proposition in its day, designed to bring together the best film-makers and allow them to make the movies they wished to make, guaranteeing them Rank financing and little interference, from casting to final cut. It was here that film-makers like David Lean, Michael Powell and Emeric Pressburger, Frank Launder and Sidney Gilliat, Ronald Neame and others would make their first significant movies.

The True Glory, made in 1945 by Garson Kanin and Carol Reed, proved to be the largest-scale documentary made at Pinewood during the war. A co-production between the AFPU and the American Photographic Corps and narrated by Peter Ustinov, it followed the events of the D-Day invasions and the subsequent end of the war. It was considered such a significant production that Colonel Frank Capra was sent over to supervise its post-production.

The events it captured showed the world how the war had been won. Now that the fighting was over, it was time for servicemen and women to come home, and for film studios in Britain to return to doing what they had been built for in the first place.

The story of YOUR victory... told by YOUR guys who won it!

Gen. Dwight D. Eisenhower's

The TRUE GLORY

Directed by
Capt. GARSON KANIN (FOR THE UNITED STATES) · CAROL REED (FOR GREAT BRITAIN)
Distributed by COLUMBIA PICTURES
FOR OFFICE OF WAR INFORMATION
THROUGH WAR ACTIVITIES COMMITTEE · MOTION PICTURE INDUSTRY

AFTER THE WAR –
UP AND ROLLING AGAIN

I N THE YEARS FOLLOWING THE WAR, key film-makers and performers would start to emerge through the stages of Pinewood and Shepperton. From directors such as David Lean to hugely popular comedians like Norman Wisdom, for the next decade or more, these studios would deliver movies that would keep the country flocking to the cinema and find great success around the world. More than anything during this period it was comedy that kept the studios alive and thriving – from Wisdom to Betty Box and Ralph Thomas and their Doctors, to the antics of the girls of St Trinian's through to the beginning of the Carry On run, the nation needed to laugh, and Rank and Korda were determined to make sure there was product to make them do just that.

But before any of that could get going, both men set about upgrading their equipment. The technology of the industry had progressed in the years in which the studios had lain relatively dormant, and Rank in particular, after what he had seen of his American counterparts in his recent visit to Hollywood, knew the UK facilities had to be upgraded.

Shepperton was the first to open for business again, in September 1945 (Pinewood would follow a few months into the following year), and it was a Rank production that was the first to shoot there. Unfortunately, *London Town* was not one of the producer's finest moments. Once again encouraged by what he had seen in Hollywood, Rank wanted to produce a large-scale British musical, something for which he thought a post-war country would have a huge appetite. He went so far as to fly in Hollywood director Wesley Ruggles to helm the film. The Hollywood veteran complained about the state of the production facilities at the studios. The film proved to be a major flop, with Rank later describing it as one of his 'biggest mistakes'.

He was, however, finding plenty of success elsewhere, most notably through the work of his Independent Producers Ltd. This period saw the emergence of some of Britain's premiere film-makers, doing some of their finest work and establishing themselves on the global stage. Frank Launder and Sidney Gilliat were the first of this group into production with their thriller *Green for Danger*. They were quickly followed by David Lean with the first of his acclaimed Charles Dickens adaptations, *Great Expectations*, which began shooting at Denham but relocated to Pinewood to make use of its large exterior water tank, that had been built shortly after the war.

The movie was a great success and was nominated for five Oscars, including two for Lean as director and co-writer. The film-maker opted to stick with Dickens for his next film, 1948's *Oliver Twist*, shot entirely on set at Pinewood. Alec Guinness, who had taken a supporting role in *Great Expectations*, actively campaigned for the key role of Fagin. Lean himself thought the actor was completely wrong for the part, until Guinness donned full make-up for a screen test and convinced him.

A massive casting call went out to find Lean's Oliver, and from some 1,500 children auditioned, the eight-year-old John Howard Davies won the role, a part with which he would remain indelibly linked for the rest of his life, despite going on to find great success as a producer and director on the likes of *Monty Python's Flying Circus* and *Fawlty Towers*.

Whilst Lean was converting the sound stages of Pinewood into Victorian England, Michael Powell and Emeric Pressburger were busy transforming the backlot and gardens into the Himalayas for their *Black Narcissus*. This melodrama starred Deborah Kerr and was shot in glorious Technicolor by Jack Cardiff, who picked up an Oscar for his work.

John Mills and Co. have their final touches before starting a scene in David Lean's *Great Expectations* (1946).

PRECEDING PAGE: By the early 1950s, Norman Wisdom was making Pinewood his home in a series of hugely popular comedies, here hanging precariously in 1956's *Up in the World*.

FROM LEFT TO RIGHT: Moore
Marriott, Rosamund John, Jean
Simmons, Valerie Hobson, J. Arthur
Rank, Patricia Roc, Judy Campbell,
Jean Kent, Stewart Grainger, Sally
Gray, Peter Groves and John Mills at
Pinewood in 1946.

David Lean strides forth on the set of *Great Expectations* (1946), the first of his Dickens adaptations.

Powell's decision to forgo shooting *Black Narcissus* on location in India, resulted in a remarkable-looking movie certainly, but the director did regret his decision to a degree, as he recounted years later in his autobiography. 'At the next full meeting of Independent Producers, with Arthur Rank in the chair, we disclosed our plans. Everybody was delighted. It meant that the studio would be fully occupied for the first year of its peacetime operation, and since most of our work would be on the lot, it left stage space free for the others. I was caught. My own personal integrity and my horse sense had betrayed me. I was trapped in a studio complex. Instead of battling my way up Machu Picchu, surrounded by thousands of Indians, my unit panting in the rear, I would be painting the Himalayas on glass! I was never again to have such an opportunity to extend my horizons.'

Rank, however, was so impressed with the finished picture that he took a print to Hollywood on his next visit and screened it for all the studio heads there.

Powell and Pressburger meanwhile continued their remarkable adventures in Technicolor with their next production, *The Red Shoes*. Pressburger had written

Michael Powell opted to bring the mountain to Pinewood's backlot for 1947's Technicolor dream *Black Narcissus*. Deborah Kerr rings bells.

LEFT: David Lean looks down on a young John Howard Davies, Alec Guinness and cast in 1948's *Oliver Twist*, shot entirely at Pinewood Studios.

the story a decade earlier for Alexander Korda, who had retained the rights. Now, he and Powell had to get back the rights without alerting Korda, who already had his eye on Rank's Independent Producers.

'First we had to buy back Emeric's script from Alex,' the director recalled, 'and we took infinite pains to avoid alerting that gentleman, who would have upped the price if he knew how much we wanted it, or even refused to sell at all. We decided not to approach London Films ourselves, but to use our parent company, Independent Producers as an intermediary … Above all, this diplomat was instructed not to say that we contemplated making *The Red Shoes* our next production for Rank. We need not have worried. I have no idea at what figure of accumulated cost *The Red Shoes* stood – or should I say danced? – on the books of London Films. Certainly, Emeric had not been paid much for his original story script. But times had changed, and when a price of £18,000 was quoted, we were in no mood to argue. Alex bought another Monet, and we got on with the rewrite.'

'First we had to buy back Emeric's script from Alex, and we took infinite pains to avoid alerting that gentleman, who would have upped the price if he knew how much we wanted it.'

Michael Powell on wresting *The Red Shoes* away from Alexander Korda

That rewrite would go on to earn Pressburger an Oscar nomination; *The Red Shoes* was also nominated for Best Picture, and won for both Best Art Direction and Best Music.

The recently knighted Sir Alexander Korda had returned to the UK during the war with the express intention of purchasing Shepperton Studios, which he did in April of 1944, paying £380,000 for a 74 per cent stake. This put him in the same league as his rival J. Arthur Rank, who had purchased Korda's beloved Denham out from under him just a few years before. With the purchase of Shepperton came the studios at Worton Hall, where the film-maker had often worked before the war, and which now became a companion studio to Shepperton, with production often crossing between the two.

Korda established his offices in a mansion on the corner of Hyde Park, but lived in a penthouse at Claridge's, where he lavishly entertained colleagues from the film industry and other wealthy and influential figures of the day.

His brother Vincent oversaw the refitting and upgrading of the studios, and Alexander began with a typically ambitious production slate. Whilst Powell and Pressburger were busy building the Himalayas on the backlot at Pinewood for

Michael Powell, Emeric Pressburger and their cinematographer Jack Cardiff brought glorious Technicolor to Pinewood and Moira Shearer in 1948's *The Red Shoes*.

Orson Welles talks Harry Lime with
his director, Carol Reed, on the set
of 1949's Academy Award-winning
The Third Man.

Black Narcissus, Korda was asphalting the grounds at Shepperton to recreate a full-scale Hyde Park Corner (more or less the view from his office) for his return to directing – his take on Oscar Wilde's *An Ideal Husband*.

The movie did not prove to be the hit that Korda had originally hoped for, but he found far greater success shortly afterwards in recreating the sewers of Vienna for Carol Reed's *The Third Man*. The movie's star, an imported Orson Welles, proved to be as elusive as his iconic character Harry Lime during production, with Vincent Korda being dispatched to Rome and Venice to track down the fleeing star and drag him back to complete his work at Shepperton.

Having originally flirted with Rank, Hollywood mogul David O. Selznick had instead opted to go with Korda and partnered with him on *The Third Man*. A huge success upon release, the film secured an Oscar nomination for Reed, who was knighted shortly after, an honour said to have been secured largely through Korda's social influence.

Orson Welles proved to be as elusive as his iconic character Harry Lime, with Vincent Korda being dispatched to Rome and Venice to track down the fleeing star and drag him back to complete his work at Shepperton.

However, despite the ambition of the film-makers, the quality of the films being produced and their success – not to mention the awards they were garnering on the world stage – the years following the war were a time of great insecurity for the British film industry. To get the country out of its financial crisis, the government needed to decrease imports and increase exports – and Hollywood movies were seen as a major import, with the majority of their earnings leaving the country. To deal with this, an *ad valorem* tax was introduced, which imposed a duty on US movies at 75 per cent. Rank was in the US attempting to set up distribution deals when news of this broke, and saw first hand how unpopular it was, with his deals collapsing in response.

Within three days, the Motion Picture Association of America (MPAA) reacted, swiftly embargoing the transport of all movies into the UK. In the eyes of the government this was a good means of buoying up the market for British films and ensuring profits stayed in the country. But the reality was that British film production had only just restarted on any great scale, and there was simply not enough indigenous product to meet the demand.

On his return to England, Rank attempted to address the matter by announcing a new slate of forty-seven productions to begin almost immediately. Again, though, the

Michael Powell and Emeric Pressburger pose during the making of 1943's *One of Our Aircraft is Missing*.

logistics of film production meant that the immediate demand would still not be met. The debacle was exacerbated in March of 1948, when future prime minister Harold Wilson, then in his role as President of the Board of Trade, made a deal with the MPAA, lifting the 75 per cent duty on US movies. The result was an influx of glamorous and exciting American movies into the country, which quickly took dominance over British films in the marketplace, leaving both Rank and Korda in great financial difficulty. Having pledged to make a large number of films to fill the gap that was no longer there, Rank found himself in the region of £16 million in debt.

Unfortunately, these were not the only woes he was facing. Eager to expand and diversify, Rank explored numerous other avenues during this period, the majority of which led to further losses.

The likes of Diana Dors, Jill Ireland, Christopher Lee and Joan Collins all passed through the doors of what became known as the Rank Charm School.

He attempted to launch a British animation unit to rival Disney, which would make films initially designed for a British audience. To this end he brought over leading Disney animator David Hand to head up production. The unit folded with losses of around half a million pounds. A similar attempt to forge a children's film unit also floundered. The idea was subsequently picked up by the government a few years later, when the Children's Film Foundation would be formed, destined to bring many hours of pleasure to Saturday-morning cinema clubs up and down the land. Ironically, J. Arthur Rank was made its chairman.

One of Rank's most heartfelt disappointments during this period was a series of topical documentary shorts entitled *The Modern Age* (each one ended with the line 'The Challenge Must Be Met in the Modern Age'), inspired by the American newsreel *The March of Time*. Rank felt very personally involved in these films, believing, as he had done with his religious films, that the cinema could educate as much as entertain. The series ran for four years but ended due to failures in distribution.

More successful was the Company of Youth, which became known as the Rank Charm School. Situated in Highbury, north London, this was a studio where young talent were selected and nurtured for further success in the movies. Actors were contracted on a renewable yearly basis and paid £20 per week. Looks played as large a part as talent, and during the studio's lifetime, the likes of Diana Dors, Jill Ireland, Christopher Lee and Joan Collins passed through its doors. But the Charm School was an ill-conceived idea, and whilst it did indeed produce some talented future stars, there was no direct obligation for Rank's producers to employ its talent, so it soon faded away.

David Lean lines up a shot on the set of *Great Expectations* (1946).

Lean (seated, centre) eats lunch on the hop during the filming of *Oliver Twist* (1948).

Korda was also facing financial difficulties at Shepperton but, as ever, seemed undeterred, looking to the British government and its recently formed National Film Fund Company to finance such large-scale productions as *Bonnie Prince Charlie* and *Anna Karenina*, the latter starring Vivien Leigh and Ralph Richardson.

Although Korda and Rank were friends and would occasionally socialise together, there was still a rivalry between them, and the loss of Denham continued to rankle with Korda. When Rank and Pinewood's financial downturn led to the dissolution of Independent Producers Ltd, Korda was swift to step in and offer Rank's key film-makers a new home at Shepperton. It was, after all, a move he had been quietly hoping for for quite some time, as Michael Powell recalled in his autobiography. 'We were seeing a good deal of Alex. He had already begun his campaign to break up Rank's Independent Producers,' he recounted. 'We were alumni of London Films, and he behaved as if we still were his darling chicks. We were asked to dinner not once, but often, to the fabulous penthouse apartment at the top of Claridge's where Alex lived and entertained.

'These little dinners at Claridge's were very pleasant and gradually whittled away our single-minded loyalty to Arthur Rank. I never noticed it, but no doubt Emeric did. He knew Alex. I only knew that it was pleasant to be treated as an equal, by a great gambler in the great world of international films … He never made the slightest attempt to undermine our loyalty to Arthur. He made gentle fun of him, he flattered us and bided his time.

'I have said enough to show how desirable a prey Independent Producers must have seemed to Alex. He saw himself as head of this group of box-office conjurors – like Denham, only bigger and better.'

Powell and Pressburger did indeed leave Rank's Pinewood to relocate at Korda's Shepperton. They were joined shortly afterwards by David Lean, who brought his production of *The Sound Barrier* over to Korda's studios. John and Roy Boulting were also brought into the fold when Korda backed their ambitious thriller *Seven Days to Noon*. (The Boulting Brothers would go on to make a number of social dramas and comedies at the studios over the next several years.)

Just over a decade earlier, Rank had been at the peak of his success, buying Denham from Korda. Now their roles were being reversed. As Rank struggled to keep Pinewood and his empire afloat, Korda was in the ascendant, with many of Rank's star film-makers now under his auspices at Shepperton. Both Denham Studios and Worton Hall closed in 1951, but Korda continued to expand, opening E, F and G stages at Shepperton in 1953.

Just a few years after the war, there remained a strong appetite amongst British cinemagoers to reflect on these recent events, and movies such as *The Wooden Horse*, *The Colditz Story* and *Reach for the Sky*, the biopic of war hero Douglas Bader, as played so memorably by Kenneth More, became significant hits at the box office.

But more than anything, audiences sought release from both the memory of the war and the still-rationed world around them. Whilst American movies continued to dominate the domestic box office, it became clear that in order to survive, British cinema had to find its own form. It had to be cheap. And it had to be cheerful. The home-grown British comedy movie was the natural solution, and over the next decade, both Pinewood and Shepperton delivered not only the most popular comedies of their day, but some of the most beloved and enduring British films of all time.

After an impoverished childhood and a stint in the army, Norman Wisdom had developed his lovable form of slapstick into a hugely successful music hall/variety theatre act. He was, as they say, wowing them in the West End in *Paris to Piccadilly* at the Prince of Wales Theatre when in 1952 the Rank organisation came calling with a then unprecedented seven-picture contract. And all that without even a screen test.

When Norman did eventually head out to Pinewood to film a screen test, he felt the material wasn't right for him. Although his subsequent films would always contain a romantic element, this first test played him as too much of a straight romantic lead. The comic later described it by saying, 'What sort of test was that for a comedian?'

After some initial trepidation on both sides, Wisdom was cast in his first film for Pinewood, *Trouble in Store*, in which he played a lowly department store stock boy with aspirations of becoming a window dresser and hopes of winning the girl of his dreams from the record department. It set the template for the series of Wisdom films that were to follow, fully utilising the actor's innate charm and likeability as well as his physical comedy genius, all mixed in with a touch of romance, a large dollop of pathos and a soppy song or two.

Still, the studio was nervous of such an investment and insisted the movie be tested at a screening at Camden's Gaumont. They need not have worried – the film played brilliantly, as it did on its hugely profitable theatrical run, establishing Wisdom as one of Britain's best-loved film stars.

'What sort of test was that for a comedian?'
Norman Wisdom is dissatisfied with his first 'romantic lead' screen test at Pinewood

It led to a run of Wisdom comedies filmed at Pinewood over the next decade or more, delivering some of the biggest hits of the day – *Up in the World*, *The Square Peg*, *On the Beat*, *A Stitch in Time* and more. Indeed, Norman's films were so popular with the British public that they were even capable of knocking James Bond movies off the top spot at the box office when a new one opened.

Wisdom preferred to work with a team he trusted, and John Paddy Carstairs directed many of his early movies. By the third film, *Man of the Moment*, Norman had found the producer he wanted in Hugh Stewart, who had previously worked at Pinewood during the war as part of the AFPU. Together they would make several movies over the next decade.

Norman Wisdom remained one of Britain's biggest box-office draws well into the mid 1960s. He continued to play in the West End too, often filming all day and treading the boards in the evening. He temporarily put his film career on hold when he moved to Broadway to find great success in productions of *Androcles and the Lion* and *Walking Happy*. Here he was spotted for his one and only Hollywood movie role, in William Friedkin's vaudeville-set *The Night They Raided Minsky's*, which secured him an Oscar nomination for Best Supporting Actor. A whole new career beckoned for Norman in Hollywood, but instead he returned to the UK to star in

Norman Wisdom was unhappy with his initial screen test at Pinewood, feeling he was being moved into the role of romantic leading man more than comedian. Here, however, he seems only too happy to pose for the camera, messing around with co-star Michael Caridia during a break in filming of 1956's *Up in the World*.

Wisdom clowns with venerable co-star Margaret Rutherford in 1953's *Trouble in Store*, the first of Wisdom's Pinewood movies, which went on to become a huge box office success and establish the diminutive comedian as one of the most enduring comic stars of British cinema.

RIGHT: Here *Doctor in the House* (1954) star Dirk Bogarde poses with Shirley Eaton and bony friend. Producer Betty Box and her director partner Ralph Thomas were responsible for a host of comedy successes from the 1950s to the early 1970s.

an ill-advised attempt at a swinging-sixties-flavoured sex comedy, *What's Good for the Goose*. When his wife left him that same year, Wisdom, still potentially one of British cinema's biggest draws, put his career on hold to raise his children.

It was around the time that Norman Wisdom was making his debut screen test that yet another talented man took up residence at Pinewood. As much as the studio was dependent on its own Rank-backed productions, it also needed to generate income from outside renters, those who would come in and use the facilities available on site. In 1952, Walt Disney brought the Henry VIII/Mary Tudor family adventure film *The Sword and the Rose* to the studios. There was some controversy during production when he insisted on having a tea trolley on stage throughout the day, as was the way in American studios. British studio workers, however, were contractually guaranteed two full tea breaks per working day, so Disney's new style took some getting used to.

Disney was impressed with the studios and continued to make live-action movies there, often period pieces, ranging from *Swiss Family Robinson* to *In Search of the Castaways* ('A thousand thrills. And Hayley Mills', as the poster proclaimed). Even

Betty Box consults with her long-time directing partner Ralph Thomas, 1960.

LEFT: Betty Box reviews the rushes of her latest film. Box's run of comedy movies, including the hugely popular 'Doctor' series, saw her nicknamed 'Betty Box-Office'.

after his death in 1966, the Disney company retained a base at Pinewood, producing such family-friendly hits as 1975's *One of Our Dinosaurs is Missing*, all the way up to their last residential production, 1981's *Dragonslayer*. (The company that still bears Walt's name would eventually return to Pinewood many years later.)

J. Arthur Rank had developed a scheme at Pinewood that teamed producers and directors to work regularly, and therefore more effectively, together. Betty Box, who would become one of the most influential and successful female film producers of her time, had cut her teeth making propaganda films during the war, alongside her brother Sydney at Verity Films. She progressed into features and in 1949 moved to Pinewood, where she was quickly teamed with director Ralph Thomas, who had begun his career in 1932 as a clapper boy in Shepperton.

In 1954, they optioned a series of books by Dr Richard Gordon and began a run of seven films based on those books, beginning with that year's *Doctor in the House*, and remaining hugely popular up until 1970's *Doctor in Trouble*. The Doctor series served to make stars of Dirk Bogarde and Donald Sinden, and of Leslie Phillips, who took the lead in the later films, and also helped introduce Brigitte Bardot to the world, via her supporting role in the second movie, *Doctor at Sea*.

The Box–Thomas partnership remained both prolific – other non-Doctor productions included 1958's *A Tale of Two Cities* and 1959's remake of *The 39 Steps* – and profitable for Rank, so much so that Box's nickname became 'Betty Box-Office'. The producer was awarded an OBE in 1958. Ten years before that, Box married Peter Rogers, a fellow producer who himself would go on to have a significant impact on Pinewood's comedy output as the director of the soon-to-be Carry On series.

The Box–Thomas partnership remained both prolific and profitable for Rank, so much so that Box's nickname became 'Betty Box-Office'.

PRECEDING PAGE AND RIGHT: The girls of St Trinian's bike round their Shepperton home and – opposite – prepare to pounce on Alistair Sim, as he takes a break during filming of the series launcher *The Belles of St Trinian's* (1954).

Whilst Pinewood had Wisdom and Doctors, Shepperton had naughty schoolgirls, based on the darkly comic cartoons of Ronald Searle. Frank Launder and Sidney Gilliat produced a quartet of St Trinian's movies at Shepperton, beginning with *The Belles of St Trinian's* in 1954, and continuing up until *The Great St Trinian's Train Robbery* in 1966. The producing pair had previously made a school comedy with 1950's *The Happiest Days of Your Life*, and employed much of the cast of that movie in their schoolgirl quartet, with Alistair Sim playing the dual role of both the headmistress, Miss Millicent Fritton, and her brother Clarence, George Cole playing the dodgy spiv Flash Harry (forever emerging from the bushes), and Joyce Grenfell as a put-upon local policewoman.

The series was revived briefly in 1980, and more successfully in 2007, but none of the films were as well received or as well loved as Launder and Gilliat's originals.

As comedy came to dominate the output of both Pinewood and Shepperton and the demands of British audiences, there was one series that had yet to emerge. And to think it all began with a modest army comedy in 1958, starring William Hartnell and Bob Monkhouse.

Carry On Sergeant (a title in which the 'Carry On' was a simple instruction, a verb that was to become a well-loved noun) was the brainchild of producer Peter Rogers. Adapted from the R. F. Delderfield novel *The Bull Boys*, it quickly established the saucy, innuendo-laden ensemble style that would come to define the incredibly popular series, which ran for a total of thirty-one films over a period of thirty-six years and created a whole raft of British comedy stars. Although Monkhouse and Hartnell would never grace a Carry On again, this first film did introduce such series veterans as Kenneth Williams, Kenneth Connor, Charles Hawtrey, Terry Scott and Hattie Jacques. Many more would follow.

For this first outing, producer Peter Rogers teamed up with director Gerald Thomas, the brother of Betty Box's working partner Ralph, ensuring that the Box–Rogers–Thomas families pretty much had a stranglehold on mainstream British film

comedy for many a year. Rogers and Thomas's partnership would remain in place for all thirty-one movies.

Carry On Sergeant quickly established the saucy, innuendo-laden ensemble style that would come to define the incredibly popular series, which ran for a total of thirty-one films over a period of thirty-six years.

The success of the barracks-based comedy led to the notion of a follow-up. Rather than return to the characters and milieu of the original, Rogers, Thomas and screenwriter Norman Hudis (who would remain one of the two key writers on the series, Talbot Rothwell being the other) decided to focus on other classic British institutions. And delightfully undermine them. Thus *Carry On Nurse* came next (having a pop at the National Health Service, and adding Joan Sims to the rapidly expanding troupe of semi-regular players), followed by *Carry On Teacher*, which took its customary swipe this time at education.

Sid James, who alongside Williams, Connor, Hawtrey and, later, Barbara Windsor formed the nexus of the Carry On players, came on board with the fourth film, *Carry On Constable*.

Whilst continuing to poke fun at British institutions – the Empire in *Carry On Up the Khyber* (1968) and trade unions (and toilets!) in 1971's *Carry On at Your Convenience*, for example – during its heyday, which featured for the most part the 'classic' cast combination and lasted the majority of the 1960s, the Carry On series parodied popular movies of the day. From the Burton–Taylor *Cleopatra* (*Carry On Cleo*, which made use of the sets built for the abandoned shooting of the Hollywood epic at Pinewood) and the James Bond movies (*Carry On Spying*, which introduced Barbara Windsor to the team) to the success of the Hammer horrors (*Carry On Screaming*), as well as cutting a swathe through British history, from monarchy (*Carry On Henry*) to piracy (*Carry On Jack*) to highwaymen (*Carry On Dick*), whilst also taking time to look further afield, from the French Revolution (*Carry On Don't Lose Your Head*) to the American Western (*Carry On Cowboy*.) As the series progressed, it found humour in both the Brits abroad (*Carry On Abroad*, filmed entirely in England) and at home (*Carry On Camping*).

Making her debut in 1964's *Carry On Spying*, Barbara Windsor became one of the most beloved stars of the series, here seen traipsing through the mud on the backlot of Pinewood for 1969's *Carry On Camping*.

Occasionally the producers would bring in a big-name star and lose their way – as was the case with former Sergeant Bilko Phil Silvers in 1967's *Carry On Follow That Camel*. But overall the series remained incredibly popular up until the early 1970s, when not only were audiences changing – and Carry On budgets appeared to be dwindling – but misjudged attempts at remaining contemporary, such as 1978's *Carry On Emmannuelle*, saw the Carry Ons fall from favour.

The epic production of *Cleopatra* would largely be shot at Rome's Cinecittà Studios, but cameras first rolled at Pinewood in 1960, before its lead actress, Elizabeth Taylor, was taken ill and production was both delayed and relocated. Some of the elaborate sets constructed on the studio's backlot would later be used for *Carry On Cleo* (1964).

Different girls (from the *St Trinian's* mob), different bikes, different studio – but Charles Hawtrey still found himself on the run in *Carry On Doctor* (1967) as the hugely successful Carry On series set up shop at Pinewood.

Carry On Cowboy started shooting in July of 1965, was completed in September, and was on screens by November of that same year. And then they rapidly moved on to the next one.

The films proved remarkably cheap to make (stars such as Williams would complain how little they were paid), and Rogers and Thomas had them down to an almost conveyor-belt process at Pinewood. *Carry On Cowboy*, for example, started shooting in July of 1965, was completed in September, and was on screens by November of that same year. And then they rapidly moved on to the next one.

Originally owned by Anglo Amalgamated Film Distributors Ltd, the Carry Ons only actually became Rank properties from 1966 onwards. The initial response was to drop the 'Carry On' prefix from the likes of *Don't Lose Your Head* and *Follow That Camel* (with the subsequent *Carry On Doctor* originally being penned under the title *Nurse Carries On Again*). However, this was soon deemed to be detrimental to the potential box office and the movies in question were quickly rebranded as official Carry Ons.

By 1976's *Carry On England*, the series was on its last legs. Sid James had sadly died shortly before filming and Patrick Mower was cast in his place. The Rank Organisation, showing their diminishing faith in the series, refused to fully fund the production, forcing Rogers and Thomas to dip into their own pockets. Although as economical as ever – it took only a month to film – on completion it was awarded an 'AA' certificate, which would have restricted those that could see it (no one under the age of fourteen) and remove the Carry Ons from what had always been, despite their risqué nature, a family audience.

The film was recut to secure a more family friendly 'A', but by then the Rank Organisation had lost faith altogether and pulled out of any further productions.

Still based at Pinewood, however, Rogers and Thomas then attempted to catch the mood of the soft-porn element that had recently started to cross over into mainstream British cinema, by casting *Emmanuelle* star Sylvia Kristel opposite Kenneth Williams and, this time embracing the 'AA' certificate, making *Carry On Emmannuelle*, which proved to be the death knell for the series.

Reports of Carry On's death proved to be (albeit briefly) exaggerated fourteen years later, when the series was revived, once again filming at Pinewood, for *Carry On Columbus* (one of three Columbus-themed movies that year). Rogers and Thomas were in place, Jim Dale and Bernard Cribbins returned, and there was a considered attempt to create a modern equivalent of the original ensemble, with the likes of

Sid James (seen here with series producer Peter Rogers), asks, 'Why the long face?' whilst shooting 1965's *Carry On Cowboy* not way out west, just out in Iver Heath.

The Carry On ensemble assemble – including such leading lights as Barbara Windsor, Charles Hawtrey, Sid James, Joan Sims, Kenneth Williams, Kenneth Connor, Bernard Bresslaw, Peter Butterworth and more, for 1972's *Carry On Abroad*.

Julian Clary, Rik Mayall, Maureen Lipman, Peter Richardson, Alexei Sayle and more. Sadly, lightning did not strike a thirty-first time.

Despite their ignominious end, the Carry On movies remain some of the best-loved films ever produced at Pinewood. During their time, Rogers and Thomas created a film-making paradigm that J. Arthur Rank would have been proud of – quickly produced, cheaply budgeted films that (whilst never much of a critical success) brought pleasure to millions over many years. And certainly helped keep Pinewood in business.

Not that it was all laughs at either studio during this period. By now, John Davis was in charge of the day-to-day running of Pinewood. A former accountant for Oscar Deutsch, Davis rose rapidly in the company and became managing director of the Rank Organisation and a close confidante of J. Arthur himself. With a strict adherence to keeping budgets low and productions on schedule, the organisation was beginning to turn around its previous financial difficulties, helped greatly by its constant run of comedies, all of which fell into Davis's design for low-budget mass entertainment.

A Night to Remember was the largest and most expensive production made to date at Pinewood, and coincided with the studio's twenty-first-birthday celebrations in 1957.

However, outside of the world of comedy, the studio was producing some outstanding dramas. One of the most significant of these was a film that tackled the tragedy of the sinking of the *Titanic*. Made in 1958, *A Night to Remember* brought together an all-star cast and uniquely impressive special effects and model work to tell this hugely emotive story.

The film was the largest and most expensive production made to date at Pinewood (and coincided with the studio's twenty-first-birthday celebrations). The large-scale model of the ship used for the sinking scenes was thirty-five feet long and had to be built in sections, as the tank it was being filmed in was not deep enough to accommodate it in its entirety.

For the scenes featuring the rescue of the survivors, there was no tank big enough at the studios; instead the production decamped to Ruislip Lido, a large outdoor swimming area, and shot through the night. When leading man Kenneth More saw how reluctant the extras were to jump into the water at two o'clock in the morning, he took it upon himself to get things moving. 'Never had I experienced such cold in all my life,' the actor recalled. 'It was like jumping into a deep freeze just like the

Sid James gives us his Henry VIII with Barbara Windsor in 1971's *Carry On Henry,* the twenty-first Carry On film.

LEFT AND FOLLOWING PAGE:
The sinking of the *Titanic* was
recreated on the Paddock Tank
at Pinewood – although the ship
proved too big for the backlot and
had to be built in sections for 1958's
all-star *A Night to Remember*.

'I recall driving out to Pinewood at night. When I drove around the backlot, there was the *Titanic*, right against the skyline, fully lit. I'll never forget that sight. I couldn't believe how big it was.'

David McCallum arrives on the set of *A Night to Remember*

people did on the actual *Titanic*. The shock of the cold water forced the breath out of my lungs. My heart seemed to stop beating. I felt crushed, unable to think. I had rigor mortis … without the mortis. And then I surfaced, spat out the dirty water and, gasping for breath, found my voice. "Stop!" I shouted. "Don't listen to me! It's bloody awful! Stay where you are!" But it was too late as the extras followed suit.'

David McCallum was a young contract actor at Rank when he was offered a small role in *A Night to Remember*. Like More, he remembers the cold of the lido, but more for the fact that he made his wife, the actress Jill Ireland, scream when he got into bed after the night's shoot. 'It was because I was a block of ice,' the actor later recollected. 'I had been in the water all night when we were shooting at Ruislip Lido and it was only ten degrees warmer in Ruislip than it was in the Atlantic. When I had been in that water it was nice and warm. In fact, it feels warmer and warmer and warmer until it feels like you're boiling. However, what these symptoms mean is that you're actually freezing to death.'

McCallum also remembered seeing the model of the ship itself on the water tank of Pinewood, one of his first experiences of working at the studios. 'I recall driving out to Pinewood at night. I knew they had been building a large piece of the *Titanic* set on the lot. When I drove around the backlot, there it was, right against the skyline, fully lit. I'll never forget that sight. Just seeing that ship up on the horizon. I couldn't believe how big it was.'

Richard Attenborough had begun his association with Pinewood when he was stationed there as part of the RAF Film Unit during the war, before subsequently finding fame as an actor in John Boulting's 1947 adaptation of Graham Greene's *Brighton Rock*. By the late 1950s, he had formed Beaver Films with writer and actor Bryan Forbes. They worked between Pinewood and Shepperton, filming their hard-hitting social drama *The Angry Silence* at the latter. Along with the likes of John Osborne's *Look Back in Anger*, the movie ushered in a new era of social realism in British cinema. Forbes would turn director with 1961's *Whistle Down the Wind*, shot on location and at Pinewood and starring Hayley Mills – this time without the thousand thrills, but with Alan Bates as a convict on the run. Beaver Films would return to the gritty determination of *The Angry Silence* the following year with its adaptation of Lynne Reid Banks' *The L-Shaped Room*, also shot at Shepperton. Both film-makers would return to these studios again and again throughout their

Richard Attenborough and Bryan Forbes' production company, Beaver Films, shot many of their often socially conscious movies at Pinewood and Shepperton. Here they flank director Guy Green and actress Pier Angeli, to display their recent awards for 1960's *The Angry Silence*.

RIGHT: The Mills sisters – 15-year-old Hayley and her 19-year-old big sister Juliet (seated) – found themselves working on two different films at Pinewood at the same time, in 1960. Child star Hayley was filming *Whistle Down the Wind* for Forbes and Attenborough, whilst Juliet was preparing to take the title role in *My Darling Daughter*.

careers, with Attenborough in particular favouring Shepperton, where he made such later works as *Chaplin*, *Cry Freedom*, *Shadowlands* and his multi-Oscar-winning *Gandhi* in 1982.

In 1953, an American producer had relocated to the UK to make a war movie called *The Red Beret*, with Alan Ladd. He shot this, his first film in the UK, at Shepperton. But his subsequent work would become synonymous with Pinewood Studios. His name was Albert R. Broccoli.

THE NAME'S BOND

JUST AS PINEWOOD HAD DOMINATED the mood of the nation with its comedies of the 1950s, so it would shape the world-view of the 1960s with James Bond, ushering in the era of what would become known as the modern blockbuster.

Creator of James Bond, Ian Fleming had served with British Naval Intelligence during World War II and called upon his wartime experiences when writing about the character of agent 007, licensed to kill. The first of Fleming's fourteen Bond books, *Casino Royale*, was published in 1953. It initially attracted some interest from film-makers, although Betty Box was one who passed on it. At the time Pinewood's contract producer, Ian Hunter took an option on Fleming's third novel, *Moonraker*, in 1955 but proved unable to get the project off the ground. Fleming and his agent bought back the rights in 1959.

Someone else who tried to acquire the rights to Bond during this period was American producer Albert Romolo Broccoli.

Born in Queens, New York, on 5 April 1909, Broccoli – nicknamed 'Cubby' from an early age – began his career as a theatrical agent before moving into producing, having teamed with fellow producer Irving Allen to form Warwick Films in the early 1950s. Relocating to the UK, Broccoli and Allen made their first movie in 1953 (the same year Fleming published *Casino Royale*). The World War II drama *The Red Beret* brought over American leading man Alan Ladd and was shot at Shepperton.

Cubby saw the potential in the Bond books very early on, but his partner was less convinced. Attempting to secure the rights, he found they were by now owned by Canadian producer Harry Saltzman. With Saltzman unwilling to sell, Broccoli persuaded him to go into partnership, and the two set up EON Productions (it stood for 'Everything Or Nothing') to begin the work of bringing James Bond to the big screen. Despite some initial trepidation on the producers' part that the books had by now been around for several years without being snapped up by Hollywood, Broccoli managed to secure $1 million in financing from United Artists towards adapting Fleming's sixth novel, *Dr No*.

Casting, of course, was always going to be crucial to the success of James Bond, and several up-and-coming and well-established stars of the day were considered, including the likes of Patrick McGoohan (already playing a spy on TV's *Danger Man*), David Niven (who would later play James Bond in the unofficial *Casino Royale*) and Roger Moore (who would eventually take over the lead for seven of the EON Bonds).

However, it was a relative unknown, Sean Connery, an actor with a distinctive Scottish accent, who landed the coveted role. Edinburgh-born Connery had worked as everything from a milkman to a lifeguard to a lorry driver to a coffin polisher, before taking part in the Mr Universe contest. This in turn led to an offer of theatre work, and the fledgling actor soon found himself in the chorus of *South Pacific*.

He soon started landing small TV parts and the occasional supporting role in low-budget features, most notably *Another Time, Another Place* (opposite Lana Turner), followed by the lead in the Disney fantasy *Darby O'Gill and the Little People*.

Broccoli and Saltzman saw something in him. As Broccoli once succinctly put it, 'Sean had the balls for the part.'

Right from the off, both producers had decided to ensure that the Bond series would appeal to an international audience. In the late 1950s and early 1960s, international air travel was still unavailable to the majority. One of the things the Bond movies would do was to take audiences to exotic worldwide locations they couldn't yet get to themselves. It's a trait the series has maintained for over fifty years.

Series producers Harry Saltzman and Albert 'Cubby' Broccoli first brought Ian Fleming's James Bond to the big screen with 1962's *Dr No*. That one movie spawned a franchise that would run for fifty years and counting, becoming cinema's most successful and enduring film series.

PRECEDING PAGE: Sean Connery's James Bond finds himself at the mercy of Gert Fröbe's Auric Goldfinger – 'Do you expect me to talk?' 'No, Mr Bond – I expect you to die!'

Sean Connery and Shirley Eaton on the set of 1964's *Goldfinger*.

Ken Adams' revolutionary designs for *Dr No* would make him one of the most influential production designers in cinema history.

Sean Connery and Ian Fleming, on the set of the first Bond movie, *Dr No* (1962).

To get this first Bond outing rolling, Broccoli brought back his *Red Beret* director, Terence Young, and screenwriter Richard Maibaum. They also brought on board talented young set designer Ken Adam, a man whose bold visual style and huge, impressive sets would come to define the look of the series.

The designer soon came to embrace the scope of the studio he found himself working at, adapting his sets appropriately, most notably with the lair of Dr No, and leading to a series of revolutionary designs that would make him one of the most influential production designers in cinema history. Adam's complete budget for the *Dr No* set was originally £14,000. It would eventually rise to a still extremely reasonable (given what he delivered) £21,000.

Dr No – made with no guarantee of a follow-up – nonetheless introduced many of the tropes that would define what was to become cinema's longest-running and most financially successful franchise: Bond's supporting team of M (Bernard Lee) and Miss Moneypenny (Lois Maxwell); the exotic globe-trotting locations (in this case Jamaica); and plenty of action and groundbreaking stunts. In addition, *Dr No* debuted the now immortal James Bond theme by Monty Norman, as well as the first of what would become a series of powerful and distinctive scores by John Barry, music that would prove to be so pivotal to the series.

Also introduced in *Dr No* was the first Bond girl, in this case making a star of Swiss beauty Ursula Andress – emerging from the water in a white bikini with a hunting knife.

The movie was a massive hit worldwide, making a huge star of Connery. This was followed by the next James Bond film, an adaptation of Fleming's fifth book, *From Russia With Love*.

Both Young and Maibaum returned for a movie that was to up the ante on its predecessor. This second iteration introduced a few more of what would become pivotal Bond elements, most notably the arrival of Desmond Llewelyn's Q (although officially known as Boothroyd in this particular outing), present for the first time to supply Bond with the latest advances in high-tech gadgetry.

From Russia With Love also debuted another pair of elements crucial to the ongoing success of the Bond series – the pre-credit stand-alone action sequence and, of course, the opening song, something that would become a major, and much-loved, element of the Bond franchise.

Pinewood itself also got to play a role on screen in *From Russia With Love*, with the administration block standing in for the headquarters of Bond's arch-nemesis, SPECTRE (an organisation still playing a part in the franchise to this very day).

'Prior to becoming an actor, Connery had worked as everything from a milkman to a lifeguard to a lorry driver to a coffin polisher, before taking part in the Mr Universe contest.'

Connery and Claudine Auger take to the water tank at Pinewood for the fourth 007 outing, 1965's *Thunderball*.

By the time of the third movie, *Goldfinger*, in 1964, the template was set, with an evil larger-than-life villain in Gert Fröbe's Goldfinger, distinctive henchmen (Harold Sakata's Oddjob), the glamour of worldwide locations, a theme song as individual and long-lasting as the film itself (Shirley Bassey's 'Goldfinger') and *femme fatale* Bond girls.

Plus, as ever, there was a fine line in humour, delivered by Connery with charming, note-perfect deadpan: 'Shocking. Positively shocking', on his electrocution of one of the henchmen.

And lest we forget, as the movies developed, so did the gadgets, with *Goldfinger* debuting Bond's most iconic and enduring accessory – the tricked-out Aston Martin DB5.

Maibaum was still in charge of the screenplay, but Guy Hamilton stepped into the director's chair this time, and as Bond got bigger, so did the scale of its production and the demands it placed on Pinewood. Ken Adam built the exterior of Fort Knox on the backlot of the studio, at that point the largest exterior set ever constructed at Pinewood, at a cost of £104,000, showing just how far things had come from the £14,000 total budget he was offered just three years before for *Dr No*. As he had recently shown in his work on Stanley Kubrick's *Dr Strangelove*, Adam was in his element creating supposed real-life environments strictly from his imagination – just as the War Room in *Dr Strangelove* is completely a construct (albeit one that has often been presumed to be real), so Adam's interior of Fort Knox (built on a Pinewood sound stage) bears no relation to the real thing; he had never even seen a photo of the place.

Another scene in *Goldfinger* was responsible for Connery developing his lifelong love of golf, the actor having to learn the game for the sequence where he challenges Fröbe's Goldfinger, which was shot at Stoke Park golf course, a few miles north of Pinewood.

The fourth Bond movie, *Thunderball*, largely decamped from Pinewood for the climes of the Bahamas, but the production was still based overall at what had

Painting the perfect Bond girl –
Shirley Eaton goes gold for her big
moment in *Goldfinger*, 1964 (with a
little help from make-up artist Paul
Rabiger).

Robert Helpmann became the stuff of childhood nightmares as the Child Catcher in Cubby Broccoli's cherished production of Ian Fleming's *Chitty Chitty Bang Bang* (1968), subsequently revived for the stage by Cubby's children Michael G. Wilson and Barbara Broccoli.

PRECEDING PAGE: 1967's *You Only Live Twice* allowed production designer Ken Adam to create his most ambitious set yet. This design drawing shows how he – literally – took the roof off Pinewood

rapidly become EON's home from home in Iver Heath.

For *You Only Live Twice*, Ken Adam designed his most elaborate set to date – the lair of arch-villain Ernst Stavro Blofeld (Donald Pleasence), housed in an extinct volcano that doubled as a missile silo, awash with hundreds of armed henchmen. He built this hugely ambitious set on a sound stage at Pinewood, opening up the roof to allow for dozens of stuntmen to abseil down into the compound for the movie's explosive climax. Its cost alone, at $1 million, was equal to the entire budget of *Dr No*.

You Only Live Twice also featured one of the series' most enduring vehicles – Bond's autogyro, nicknamed Little Nellie. The light aircraft was 'auditioned' to Broccoli and Saltzman by its inventor, Wing Commander Ken Wallis, flying it around the Pinewood backlot.

It was at this time that Cubby Broccoli took a break from Bond – and brought yet another flying vehicle to Pinewood. Although *Chitty Chitty Bang Bang* was a family-orientated musical and therefore would appear to be a significant departure for the spy-movie maker, it was based on the children's book by Ian Fleming (with *You Only Live Twice*'s screenwriter Roald Dahl and Bond regular Richard Maibaum working on the screenplay, Dahl often credited with significantly changing the film from the source book).

Dick Van Dyke, who had starred alongside Julie Andrews in the hugely successful and Oscar-winning Disney musical *Mary Poppins* a few years back, was brought over to take on the role of inventor Caractacus Potts, and *Poppins* composers Richard and Robert Sherman were recruited to provide the songs.

'I think Cubby really loved making that. He cared about it because he wanted to make a film for his children, for us, because we were all fairly young.'

Barbara Broccoli on her father's *Chitty Chitty Bang Bang*

'On *Chitty Chitty Bang Bang* I remember my sister and I were extras for a day. I was about eight,' Barbara Broccoli says. 'We were in a tiny bit in the circus scene where Dick Van Dyke, after the dance, is being chased and he's running through and there's someone throwing balls at one of the stands in the circus and we were the two kids jumping up and down. It was really amazing.

'I think Cubby really loved making that. He cared about it for a lot of reasons,' Broccoli continues. 'He cared about it because he wanted to make a film for his children, for us, because we were all fairly young. I was eight, my sister was twelve, my brother was thirteen. I think he also wanted to make it because he was very fond of Ian Fleming and it was very touching how that story came about. Ian Fleming's son Caspar, when he was a little boy, said to his dad one night, "I think you love James Bond more than you love me." And his response to that was writing *Chitty Chitty Bang Bang* for his son. So I think there's a lot of resonance to that. And Robert Helpmann as the Child Catcher is one of the most iconic images in film, and prominent in every young person's mind who's ever seen the film. Cubby had fun with the sets; he brought Gert Fröbe back to play the villain, the Baron. He had a lot of fun with it.'

Sticking for the most part with his Bond team, Broccoli also brought Ken Adam on board as production designer.

Despite its latter-day reputation as a family classic, and despite Van Dyke's statement in a press release of the time that *Chitty* would 'out-Disney Disney', the movie proved to be both a critical and a financial disappointment upon release.

'It wasn't a hit,' Barbara Broccoli remembers, 'and I think he always felt that was because at the time Disney was the stronger brand in terms of children's films and it didn't have the Disney brand on it. I think he was disappointed it wasn't a bigger financial success but I think he was very proud of the movie.'

Cubby Broccoli brought Bond
designer Ken Adam on board for
Chitty Chitty Bang Bang (1968).
Seen here is an early pre-production
design for the film.

George Lazenby steps in the role of Bond for one film and marries Diana Rigg, seen here behind the scenes, *On Her Majesty's Secret Service* (1969).

RIGHT: Sean Connery returns as Bond for one final outing in 1971's *Diamonds Are Forever*.

By the time the next Bond film rolled around, Sean Connery had moved on from the role that had made him internationally famous and, after a lengthy search, the Australian George Lazenby, a former male model, was assigned 007's licence to kill. *On Her Majesty's Secret Service* marked Lazenby's only outing in the role, but remains for many fans one of their favourite Bond movies, and an influence on such future film-makers as Christopher Nolan, who openly acknowledged his debt to the film in the snowbound sections of his *Inception* many years later.

Additionally, it saw Bond married (if only briefly) to Diana Rigg's Tracy di Vincenzo, and was the first (since *Dr No*), and to date last, not to feature an opening title song, though it made up for it with one of John Barry's finest ever scores, and Louis Armstrong's beautiful song-within-the-film, 'We Have All the Time in the World'.

Nonetheless, the points it earns in retrospect were nullified by its performance at the worldwide box office, a significant drop on all the previous, Connery-led outings, and proof to Broccoli and Saltzman (if proof were needed) that their Cold War anti-hero was not as interchangeable as they had hoped.

Sean Connery returned to the role of James Bond for one last time, with 1971's *Diamonds Are Forever*. The undeniable success of the film meant that even though Sean Connery had now left the part, James Bond would return …

In the wake of James Bond, many more came to spy at Pinewood, including Connery's good friend Michael Caine. Bond producer Harry Saltzman chose to diversify the nature of on-screen spying with 1965's *The Ipcress File*. Adapted from the book by espionage writer Len Deighton, the film confirmed Caine's rising-star status at the time, as agent Harry Palmer, an altogether more down-to-earth creation than James Bond, a man more comfortable catching a London double-decker bus than driving a gadget-laden Aston Martin.

Caine would go on to star as Palmer in two more big-screen outings, 1966's *Funeral in Berlin* and 1967's *Billion Dollar Brain*, which, in the flamboyant hands of director Ken Russell, came closer to straying into Bond's super-spy territory.

Filming more or less right next door to the James Bond movies, the Carry On team, naturally, also decided to jump on the Bond-wagon with 1964's *Carry On Spying*, marked by being the last Carry On movie shot in black and white and the first to feature series favourite-to-be Barbara Windsor.

Shepperton was also keen to get in on the spy trend, but took things altogether more seriously than the Carry On team with Martin Ritt's gritty 1965 adaptation of John le Carré's *The Spy Who Came in from the Cold*, starring a post-*Cleopatra* Richard Burton, alongside Claire Bloom.

Even British TV's most famous and beloved double act, Morecombe and Wise, felt the so-called spy-boom might be the right moment for them to make their leap to the big screen. Eric and Ernie made their first movie, spy spoof *The Intelligence Men*, in 1965. It would be the first of three movies they shot at Pinewood, but overall it was not the experience they hoped for.

'When we came to Pinewood, we thought we would meet all the big film stars,' Wise recalled in 1987. 'We did see a few in the restaurant, but Eric thought they'd all be popping by our dressing room, so he bought a big fridge and filled it full of booze. Nobody came. We were so disappointed. My biggest disappointment was on the first day on location, when I was sitting in my caravan, ready to do my first scene, and my lunch came in through the window on a paper plate. It was difficult for us not having an audience for the first time, as the filming was in a sort of void, and that's why I felt our films were a bit diluted. If we could have had an audience, and later cut them out, it would have worked so much better.'

Ken Adam pauses to admire his most elaborate set to date, *You Only Live Twice* (1967).

Eric and Ernie step out in the Pinewood gardens for their big screen debut, the 1965 spy-spoof *The Intelligence Men.* 'It was difficult for us not having an audience for the first time, as the filming was in a sort of void, and that's why I felt our films were a bit diluted. If we could have had an audience, and later cut them out, it would have worked so much better.'

Producer Harry Saltzman on the set of 1967's *Billion Dollar Brain* with director Ken Russell and stars Karl Malden and Michael Caine, cup of tea in hand.

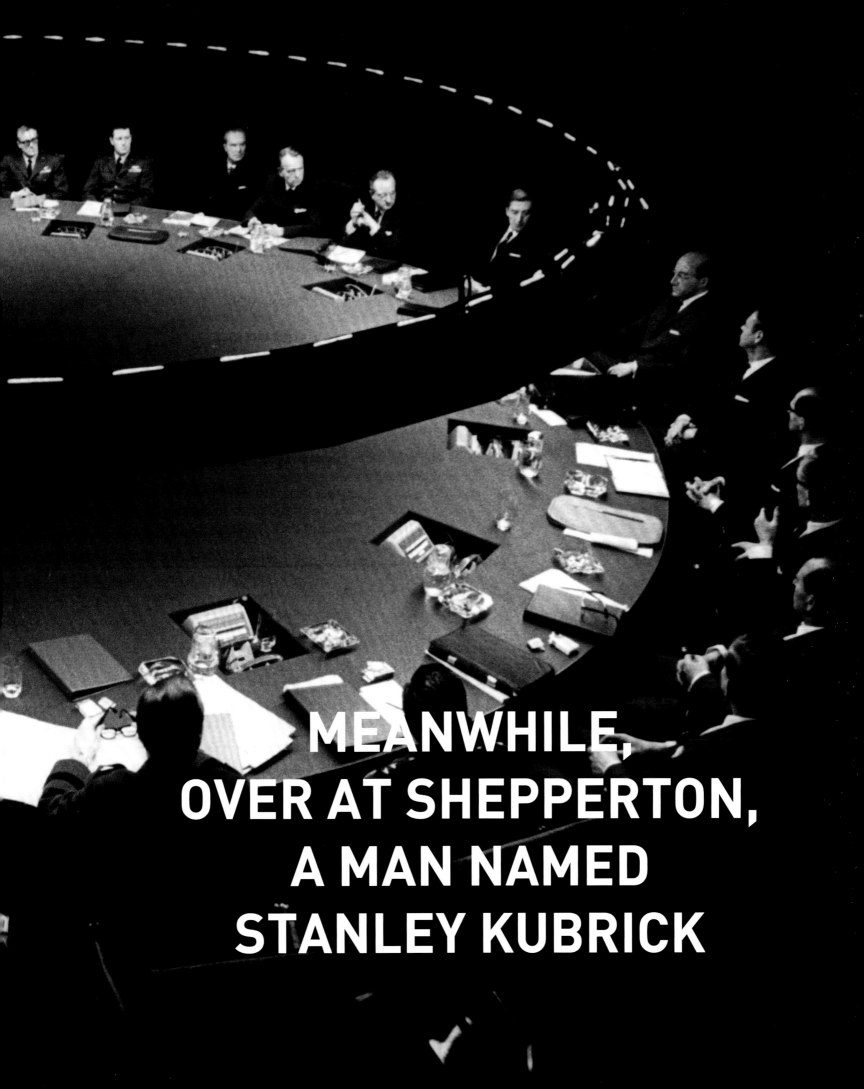

MEANWHILE,
OVER AT SHEPPERTON,
A MAN NAMED
STANLEY KUBRICK

J**UST AS CUBBY BROCCOLI** had relocated to England in the early 1950s, so would fellow New York-born film-maker Stanley Kubrick in the early 1960s. Kubrick was born in the Bronx on 28 July 1928. After an ill-starred time in school, young Stanley parlayed his love of photography into a job as a photographer for *Look* magazine in the late 1940s. Using his pay cheques from his various photo assignments, he began making short movies, often calling on family and friends to help fund such ventures.

Employing similar financing methods, he made two small independent features – 1953's *Fear and Desire* and 1955's *Killer's Kiss* – neither of which made much of a mark or, indeed, much at the box office. But they did lead to his first studio picture, 1956's *The Killing*, a noir crime drama, much acclaimed in retrospect but again something that at the time did not have the impact the director had hoped for.

The Killing, however, did serve to bring the young film-maker to the attention of Hollywood leading man Kirk Douglas, who recruited Kubrick to helm what would become his breakthrough movie, the powerful anti-war drama *Paths of Glory*.

The film was significant for Kubrick in many ways. It took him to work in Europe (it was shot on location in Germany) for the first time, introduced him to his future wife Christiane Harlan, and, most importantly, with its critical reaction, established him as a film-maker of international renown.

Furthermore, it led to Douglas replacing director Anthony Mann with the young Stanley on the large-budget epic *Spartacus* in 1960.

At the age of thirty-one, Kubrick was then the youngest director in Hollywood history to helm such an epic. But already the perfectionist film-maker was unhappy with the workings of Hollywood and clashed often with both the studio and his star, Douglas. Dissatisfied with Hollywood in general and his experiences on *Spartacus*, Kubrick decided to try working in Europe, somewhere he would remain for the majority of his subsequent life and career.

His adaptation of Vladimir Nabokov's controversial novel *Lolita*, starring James Mason and a transformative Peter Sellers, was the first film Kubrick shot primarily in the UK. Sellers himself already had a relationship with Shepperton Studios, having established himself on film – and away from the radio success of *The Goon Show* – in such Boulting Brothers productions as *Carlton-Browne of the FO* and *I'm All Right Jack*.

Following the success of *Lolita*, Columbia Pictures agreed to fund whatever it was the film-maker wanted to do next, on the proviso it feature the extraordinarily talented Sellers. Ideally in several roles.

Kubrick had left his native America in part due to his misgivings about the country's future in the midst of the Cold War and the increasing levels of violence he saw around him in American cities. He wanted to put these feelings about the uncertainty of man's future into his next picture, and had started working with author Peter George, adapting his nuclear threat novel, *Red Alert*. But as things progressed, it became more and more apparent to Kubrick that these events and likelihoods were so absurd in themselves that the only way to depict them was to become absurdist. Thus he brought on board American satirist Terry Southern, author of acclaimed comic novel *Candy*, to help pen the script.

Sellers, however, remained a necessity for financing, and with the actor refusing to travel or shoot outside the UK, it was suggested that Kubrick set up his new production at Shepperton. The director subsequently wrote to then studio head John Boulting with a list of technical questions regarding his plans for elaborate model and matte work, jokingly concluding his letter, 'PS Do you have electricity at Shepperton?'

When a strange alien monolith landed on the moon, Stanley Kubrick decided to build the moon at Shepperton – *2001: A Space Odyssey* (1968).

PRECEDING PAGE: 'Gentlemen, you can't fight in here. This is the War Room.' *Dr Strangelove or: How I Learned to Stop Worrying and Love the Bomb* (1964).

After some initial discussion about shooting the movie on colour stock – with Kubrick enquiring if England could meet his needs in terms of supply of such – it was decided to shoot the film that would become *Dr Strangelove or: How I Learned to Stop Worrying and Love the Bomb* in black and white, something that in retrospect for ever confirmed its place at the heart of Cold War cinema.

With Columbia's financing contingent on Sellers, the comic actor was originally taken on to play five roles in the movie. But Sellers' uncertainty about his ability to pull off a Texan accent led to his roles being reduced to three – and Slim Pickens picking up the part of Texan bomb-riding pilot Major T. J. 'King' Kong.

Kubrick jokingly ended his letter to studio head John Boulting by asking, 'PS Do you have electricity at Shepperton?'

Kubrick reaches out to actor Slim Pickens, who in turn gets ready to love the bomb in 1964's *Dr Strangelove.*

Impressed by his recent work on *Dr No* over at Pinewood, Kubrick enlisted Ken Adam as his production designer and, as it turned out, his de facto chauffeur, with Adam driving Kubrick out to Shepperton every day in his newly purchased E-Type Jaguar. (Although it was the fastest sports car in town, Kubrick insisted his production designer never go above 30 mph, much to the young designer's frustration.)

The highlight of Adam's work on *Strangelove* was undoubtedly the War Room of Sellers' President Merkin Muffley, where much of the action of the film's later stages takes place. It remains one of Adam's greatest creations, and became so iconic that, many years later, when he became president, former actor Ronald Reagan asked to see the War Room and was shocked (and probably disappointed) to discover it didn't exist.

Although its release was delayed from late 1963 to early 1964, due to the assassination of President John F. Kennedy, *Dr Strangelove* proved to be another success for Kubrick, who soon began work on his next project, one that would take four years to come to fruition and that would, once again, find the film-maker making use of Shepperton Studios.

Stanley Kubrick first met science fiction author Arthur C. Clarke on a return visit to his native New York in April 1964. He was initially intrigued by Clarke's short story 'The Sentinel'. Their ongoing discussions took elements of that story and developed it into what would become the groundbreaking *2001: A Space Odyssey*, with Clarke writing his novel of the film and the screenplay simultaneously, the latter with Kubrick.

By now Kubrick was a full-time resident in the UK and would once again take his

production to Shepperton – although the sheer scale of the piece (the budget of which shot up from $2 million to an unprecedented $10 million as it progressed) meant that it would also inhabit stages at MGM Borehamwood in Elstree. Filming actually began in late 1965 and continued for two years – allowing plenty of time for the movie's revolutionary visual effects to be developed. Kubrick himself took on the mantle of special photographic effects designer and director, something that would (ironically, given his status as one of the greatest film directors of all time) win him his one and only Oscar. But it was Douglas Trumbull and his team that did the majority of the work – from intense model-building to the famed psychedelic trip of the film's finale.

Impressed by his recent work on *Dr No* over at Pinewood, Kubrick enlisted Ken Adam as his production designer and de facto chauffeur, with Adam driving Kubrick out to Shepperton every day in his newly purchased E-Type Jag.

Also signing up for the odyssey was special-effects veteran Brian Johnson, who had previously worked with Gerry Anderson on such TV shows as *Fireball XL5*, *Stingray* and, most significantly, *Thunderbirds*.

'Out of the blue one day I got a call from Stanley Kubrick's secretary saying that if I wanted it, there was a job for me on a picture called *2001: A Space Odyssey*,' Johnson recalls. 'I handed in my notice with Gerry. And I went along to Elstree Studios in Borehamwood and presented myself, and I was told that Stanley was on the stage doing something and I'd got to go and see him. I walked on to the stage and the only person on stage that I could see was a painter. So I went up to him and I said, "I was told Stanley Kubrick was on this stage," and he turned round and said, "I'm Stanley Kubrick." But he was dressed like he was a painter. He was standing there amongst all these paint pots.

'This was a test set for the monolith. There were many tests. It was a stage covered in black velvet with this monolith. And he didn't like it because it was in perspex, the biggest perspex block ever cast, which are crap to make, but that's another story. So that was my first introduction to Stanley.'

Once again, Kubrick's sets were expansive and quite brilliantly designed (albeit this time without the increasingly Bond-based set designer Ken Adam), with shooting kicking off with the moon excavation sequence where the monolith is (re) discovered, the elaborate set being constructed in Shepperton's H Stage.

The War Room may not have been a place for fighting, but Kubrick displayed no qualms about hiding under President Merkin Muffley's desk on the set of *Dr Strangelove* (1963).

As ever, Kubrick had begun with a vast amount of research, including trips to NASA to ensure that his and Clarke's future vision could always be seen as an extension of reality rather than a work of pure fiction. And whilst their notion of commercial space travel (and the survival of Pan Am) is still waiting to be realised (although it is not far off if you listen to Richard Branson), their depiction of the unintentionally malevolent computer HAL – a machine that holds the lives of those around it in its metaphorical hands – was noticeably unique at the time, influencing not only subsequent science fiction writing and movies, but also the development of real-world computer technology itself (as Apple's Siri will attest, if you ask it the question 'Was your dad named HAL?').

Brian Johnson found himself working closely with Kubrick and the models the film required.

'I wound up looking after all the models,' he remembers. 'Stanley and I would stand on a stage covered in black velvet with a model on a stand and then we would photograph it. Bearing in mind, he had a photographer on the unit but he didn't use him for this. For some reason he wanted me to do this with him. I don't know why, but there you go. He did that.'

'I walked on to the stage and the only person on stage that I could see was a painter. So I went up to him and I said, "I was told Stanley Kubrick was on this stage," and he turned round and said, "I'm Stanley Kubrick." But he was dressed like he was a painter.'
2001 FX man Brian Johnson meets his director

Johnson also recalls the director's eccentricities, 'We would photograph the models, and the *Discovery* model was fifty-four feet long. We shot everything in black and white with a still camera using a special CIA Polaroid stock that's high in resolution in exactly the right spot.

'So on the stage would be Stanley, me, Geordie, who was the spark, who had knuckles on the one hand and no fingers because he'd lost them during the war, but he was a real character, and we would film this stuff.'

As groundbreaking as many of the effects were in *2001: A Space Odyssey*, some of it was down to good old-fashioned smoke and mirrors. Or, in the case of the famous shot of a pen seen floating in the weightlessness of the space bus, a pane of glass and double-sided sticky tape. 'We stuck the pen on a sheet of glass on a rotating frame,' explains Johnson. 'And it was the first time that 3M had produced double-sided tape, so we used it. The glass sheet is rotating, somebody just out of picture turning it around, winding a handle. Then when the girl goes up to the pen, she doesn't put her hand round it like you would do normally. She goes up to it and picks it up. The double-sided tape had to be stronger on the pen than it was on the glass so it didn't leave the tape on the glass. It took a good few takes to get that.'

'Stanley was fascinating because he always asked the question why? Always why this? Why that? Why the other? He didn't always know why he was asking the question because he always seemed to look like he knew what he was doing.'
Johnson on working with Kubrick

Johnson enjoyed his time working with Kubrick; he even briefly joined the director on his next film, *A Clockwork Orange*. 'Stanley was fascinating because he always asked the question why? Always why this? Why that? Why the other? He didn't always know why he was asking the question because he always seemed to look like he knew what he was doing. He wasn't very clear but he just knew if he shot the shit out of it he would wind up with something he could use as a movie.'

Yet despite his admiration and friendship for Kubrick, Johnson was aware of the mercurial side of the film-maker. 'He'd tell you, don't eat this, don't eat that. Then he'd stand on the stage and eat some horrible sausage roll. He had this wonderful smile but his eyes were absolutely black, dark, dark black eyes. You couldn't see pupils or anything, just very dark eyes and a very charming smile. He was very charming.'

2001: A Space Odyssey initially divided critics but found an audience amongst the young, who would often watch the movie whilst smoking various substances to replicate Kubrick's final Star Child birth sequence. Not for nothing was its strap line 'The Ultimate Trip'.

As noted, the film won Kubrick his one and only Oscar, but even that accolade was not enough to lure him back to his home country. Over the next three decades he would make some of the most acclaimed movies in the history of cinema, from *A Clockwork Orange* to *Barry Lyndon* to *The Shining*, always in or around the UK, even going to the extreme of recreating Vietnam in London's Docklands for *Full Metal Jacket* in 1986, such was his reluctance to either shoot on location or leave his adopted homeland.

For his final movie, *Eyes Wide Shut*, starring Hollywood's hottest couple of the moment, Tom Cruise and Nicole Kidman, Kubrick returned to Pinewood, having shot much of *Full Metal Jacke*t there. Here he took over a large part of the studio and recreated a huge section of his native New York's Greenwich Village (even sending his production designers over to the US to measure the width of the actual streets to ensure accuracy).

It was an ultra-secretive production that shot for over a year as Kubrick, whose reputation as an exacting perfectionist now rivalled that of him as a film-maker, insisted on dozens, even hundreds of takes, until he had moulded his actors to his own unique vision. At least one left (Harvey Keitel was replaced by Sydney Pollack), but many stayed for the unique opportunity.

Eyes Wide Shut proved to be Stanley Kubrick's last walk on a New York street and a British studio backlot both. He died on 7 March 1999, days after finishing editing his final film, and just before its release.

Stanley Kubrick directs fellow film-maker Sydney Pollack and Pinewood regular Tom Cruise on the set of his last film, *Eyes Wide Shut* (1999).

A NEW STAGE

T HE 1960S had proved to be a boom time for production at Pinewood, buoyed in part by the ongoing production of the Bond movies and the expansion of television production at the site. New stages were being constructed, and the studio's thirtieth anniversary brochure in 1966 boasted that 1,300 people were employed there.

Shepperton saw out the decade with such acclaimed productions as the Oscar-winning *A Man for All Seasons*, the hit musical *Oliver!* and the overblown box office disaster that was *Casino Royale*. Based on the one Fleming Bond book that EON were unable to secure the rights to, producer Charles Feldman's *Casino Royale* was designed to take on the success of the Broccoli–Saltzman Bond movies and re-dress them as an all-star comedy, featuring the likes of Peter Sellers, David Niven, Orson Welles, Woody Allen, even original Bond girl Ursula Andress. It was a tortuous production, boasting a total of five directors, and proved itself a monumental flop at the box office.

A paucity of such big movies – even the misguided ones – meant that production was drying up at Shepperton towards the end of the decade, leaving the studio more and more reliant on the continued presence of the American horror outfit Amicus. Run by producers Milton Subotsky and Max Rosenberg, the company made a string of low-budget movies at the studios, with such titles as *Dr Terror's House of Horrors* and *The House That Dripped Blood*, as well as the big-screen spin-offs of the BBC's popular teatime TV serial *Dr Who*.

At the end of 1969, EMI bought MGM's Borehamwood Studios and the ABC cinema chain, leaving the future of Shepperton at least in some doubt.

As the new decade dawned, it brought with it a financially tough time for the British film industry. Alongside dwindling production and the prohibitive nature of British taxation laws, audiences were both diminishing and changing in their tastes – for example, 1971's top-grossing film was a big-screen version of popular TV sitcom *On the Buses*, beating even Sean Connery's final outing as Bond in *Diamonds Are Forever*.

At the same time, the financially unstable British Lion, then owners of Shepperton, were being pursued by various financial bodies and investors, in part due to the value of the land the studio stood on, but also for the company's expansive and highly valued film library. When British Lion posted a net loss of over £1 million for the year 1971–2, it became even more vulnerable.

1967's chaotic *Casino Royale* – a very loose comedy take on the only Fleming 007 novel Broccoli and Saltzman were unable to secure the rights to.

PRECEDING PAGE: Roger Moore, Cubby Broccoli and Barbara Bach on the set of *The Spy Who Loved Me* (1977).

David Niven on the set of *Casino Royale* (1967).

Director Fred Zinnemann takes a break with actors John Hurt, Paul Scofield and Wendy Hiller, during the shooting of 1966's *A Man for All Seasons*. The film went on to win six Oscars the following year, including Best Picture, Best Director for Zinnemann and Best Actor for Scofield.

RIGHT: Two decades after David Lean brought Dickens' orphan to Pinewood, Carol Reed took *Oliver!* (1968) to Shepperton – this time with songs, and Oscar wins to boot.

In 1972, former stockbroker John Bentley, who had rapidly risen to become company chairman of Barclay Securities, purchased British Lion and, by default, Shepperton Studios, for £5.5 million. Productions at the studio were booked up until September of 1972, but after that its future looked decidedly uncertain, with the notion of a merger with Pinewood being discussed.

Major events were also afoot over at Pinewood, with the return of director Alfred Hitchcock after an absence of more than thirty-four years. Hitchcock had shot one of his lesser-known films, *Young and Innocent*, at the studios back in 1937, before leaving for Hollywood. He returned now with what was to prove his penultimate film, the London-set serial killer drama *Frenzy*.

Sadly, as Hitchcock was winding up production, the studio was dealt another major blow with the death of founder J. Arthur Rank on 29 March 1972, at the age of eighty-three.

Roger Moore, Julius W. Harris and director Guy Hamilton on the set of *Live and Let Die* (1973).

Despite the presence of such productions as Hitchcock's, and the last stumbling outings of the Carry On series, the 1970s were also proving a difficult time financially for Pinewood. Thankfully, the studio always had one ace in the hole – Cubby Broccoli and his ongoing 007 adventures.

'Over our fifteen-month schedule on *The Persuaders!*, we filmed in every nook and cranny of Pinewood. It was supposed to be twelve months, but with Tony Curtis, whose wonderful eccentricities ensured that there was never a dull day, we over ran a little.'

Roger Moore goes back to TV in the '70s

With Sean Connery now very definitely out of the secret agent game, Broccoli had an opportunity to recast and, to some extent, reinvent his series. Having learnt from his experience with George Lazenby, he secured the services of Roger Moore to be his new Bond. He was no stranger to Pinewood, having worked there many times over the years, most recently opposite Tony Curtis on the popular TV show *The Persuaders!*

'Over our fifteen-month schedule on *The Persuaders!*' Moore recollects, 'we filmed in every nook and cranny of Pinewood, and the adjoining Black Park. It was supposed to be twelve months, but with Tony Curtis, whose wonderful eccentricities ensured that there was never a dull day, we overran a little. I was also a producer as well as star and occasional director, so it cost me money!

'The gardens, house and lot featured extensively across the series, doubling for just about everywhere, and my own personal favourite episode is "A Death in the Family", which makes good use of the gardens and pond.'

Moore's first outing as Bond, *Live and Let Die*, signified a new, lighter tone to the movies, something that had started with *Diamonds Are Forever* and would come to define the Moore era. The actor had long been associated with the character, having been on the original, pre-Connery shortlist for the role. Or so it was thought.

'They say I was on the shortlist for *Dr No*. Curiously "they" (being the PR department) only announced that fact to the media after I'd started *Live and Let Die* – somewhat opportunely. I was certainly not aware of being on any list, but it's flattering to be wanted by anyone.'

As ever with the globe-trotting Bond, the movie shot from New Orleans to Jamaica

Roger Moore with his co-star Tony Curtis in 1970, bringing *The Persuaders!* to life.

and beyond. But the villain's shark-infested underground lair was a spectacular set built on Pinewood's D Stage and described by Moore as 'the biggest set I ever worked on'.

'My first work was on location in New Orleans for the boat chases,' he continues. 'So the size and scale of Bond was very much in evidence before I returned to Pinewood on Syd Cain's sets. No expense was spared and materials used in construction were usually the very best (and most expensive). The producers never skimped and always put the money on the screen.'

Whilst Moore appears to have played down the magnitude of taking on the role of the world's most iconic screen hero, he became keenly aware of it once the filming came to an end.

'I wasn't ever apprehensive about taking over from Sean, until I was on my way to the first press screening of *Live and Let Die*, when it suddenly struck me that I might not be liked.'

Roger Moore on being the new Bond

Director Guy Hamilton on an elaborate Pinewood set with Moore – *The Man with the Golden Gun* (1974).

'I wasn't ever apprehensive about taking over from Sean,' he explains, 'until, that is, I was on my way to the first press screening of *Live and Let Die*, when it suddenly struck me that I might not be liked. But I was very fatalistic – rather like a lady going into labour, the baby was going to arrive and no one could stop it! In the event, I think I got away with it. I also worked cheap, that's why I did seven.'

He did indeed get away with it, and there were bigger things to come. Following *The Man with the Golden Gun*, Broccoli aimed to make Bond's tenth screen outing the most spectacular of them all.

Michael G. Wilson had been spending more and more time on his father's sets.

'Mostly I was a runner and an assistant director. Then when *The Spy Who Loved Me* came, I was more involved.'

His younger sister also began to play more of an active role in the family business of Bond around this time.

'I was about seventeen, eighteen,' Barbara Broccoli recounts. 'We have a brother and sister who aren't in the business, so I don't think anything was ever given that any of us would go into the industry. I just was always around and I loved it. You have

ABOVE AND RIGHT: Unable to find a stage large enough to house three nuclear submarines, for 1977's *The Spy Who Loved Me*, Cubby Broccoli decided to build one – the 007 Stage – at the time the largest in the world.

FOLLOWING PAGE: Ken Adam thought building the inside of a volcano at Pinewood was as big as things could get. Until Cubby Broccoli asked him to design and build the 007 Stage to house a trio of nuclear submarines, seen here in early sketch form.

to remember Pinewood was such an incredible place for a child. There were lots of movies being made and the restaurant in those days was the hub of show business.

'We'd be in there when we were kids, and the Carry On people would be in there, Jack Hawkins was there. All these extraordinary, wonderful actors. We would sit there and see all this wonderful stuff happening and all these fantastic people coming in and out with costumes on and it was the most vibrant, exciting, magical place. Sadly, the restaurant doesn't function like that any more because everybody is working through lunchtime, but it was like the old Hollywood commissaries. It was so much fun. You'd see all these really fun people and not only the film stars but also directors.

I remember David Lean sitting in a chair outside his cutting room and I remember it was a cold day, and there was this one little wonderful bit of sunshine that happened to just be pouring down on one spot and David Lean had positioned his chair in there. I walked by and there was David Lean, illuminated, and he said, "Sometimes

'I remember David Lean sitting in a chair outside his cutting room and I remember it was a cold day, and there was this one little wonderful bit of sunshine that happened to just be pouring down on one spot, and he had positioned his chair in there. I walked by and there was David Lean, illuminated, he said, "Sometimes you've got to just stop and smell the roses."'

Barbara Broccoli recalls her early days at Pinewood

"A VIEW TO A KILL"
PROD.
CAM. ALAN HUME B.S.C.
DIR. JOHN GLEN
SLATE 231
TAKE 1
24TH AUGUST '84 INT-DAY

you've got to just stop and smell the roses." And I thought, oh my God, that's David Lean! There were these incredible people around. So how can you not want to keep making that atmosphere and that environment? It's amazing.'

The production of 1977's *The Spy Who Loved Me* was to for ever change the nature, and look, of Pinewood Studios. The plot involved the hijacking of nuclear submarines, and a set needed to be built that could house three full-size submarines in a water tank. Cubby Broccoli, who had recently split from his long-time production partner Harry Saltzman and was producing a Bond solo for the first time, searched far and wide to find a stage that could accommodate the film's needs. But to no avail.

'It appeared to me that it was more sane, after talking to United Artists, to explore the possibility of putting up a new stage,' he later explained to *American Cinematographer*.

Broccoli drafted in Bond production designer Ken Adam to help design what would become known as the 007 Stage, at that time the largest stage in the world. It was constructed over the next seven months above the Pinewood reservoir, at a cost of $1.65 million.

'They didn't have a big enough stage,' recalls Wilson. 'So we built it into the budget of the film. We had a twenty-five-year licence in exchange for building it. And we had first call on it.'

'It appeared to me that it was more sane to explore the possibility of putting up a new stage.'
Cubby Broccoli on building the 007 Stage, then the largest in the world

Roger Moore recalls his first impression of the new stage. 'Ken Adam's stage, housing three full-size nuclear submarines, was a sight to behold. It was in fact then the largest stage in the world. Everything about it was immense, and such was its importance to Pinewood that former Prime Minister Harold Wilson attended the opening ceremony.'

The 007 Stage was officially opened on 5 December 1976. 'We had the three submarines,' recalls Barbara Broccoli, 'and Harold Wilson was there and there was a big opening day of the stage and all that. That was a big event that I specifically remember because it was so extraordinary then – the 007 Stage.'

Unfortunately, though, despite this new facility, the next Bond movie, *Moonraker*,

Roger Moore on the set of *A View to a Kill* (1985).

was relocated to France (although James Bond would return to Pinewood for his next two outings, *For Your Eyes Only* and *Octopussy*).

The 007 Stage, meanwhile, was clearly paying for itself, with Superman's Fortress of Solitude replacing *The Spy Who Loved Me*'s submarine paddock, and Ridley Scott constructing an entire fantasy forest there for *Legend*. It was during the production of the latter, over a lunch break on 24 June 1984, that a freak electrical accident occurred and the stage burnt to the ground in a matter of minutes. With the next Bond, *A View to a Kill*, already booked in, it was rebuilt in thirteen weeks and renamed the Albert R. Broccoli 007 Stage.

A View to a Kill proved to be Moore's final outing as Bond.

'My agent and bank manager were very upset when I hung up the Walther PPK, but I knew it was time,' says Moore today. 'After all, the leading ladies were the same age as my granddaughters!

'I miss the camaraderie of the crews,' the veteran actor admits, 'and, in particular, being on set every day with Cubby Broccoli.'

Timothy Dalton was brought in to follow Moore, and he took the franchise in a grittier direction, returning to the more serious tone of the early movies. But his first outing as the secret agent, *The Living Daylights*, was to be the last Bond based at Pinewood for over a decade.

By the mid '70s, the future of Shepperton was so precarious that it led to its workers forming the Shepperton Studios Action Committee. Their first move to stop proposed changes to the studio was to secure a preservation order for various trees on the site, something that attracted the attention of the likes of Spike Milligan and Alec Guinness, and, therefore, the national press.

Among the suggestions for the studio's future at that point included selling off all the equipment to Pinewood and then leasing everything back from Rank.

An alternative plan was to close half of Shepperton's eight stages, including H Stage (which had been, before the 007 Stage, the largest stage in Europe), allowing John Bentley to do with the land whatever he wanted. Bentley's overall plan was to sell British Lion, but this was contingent on the changes he had in mind for the studio going through. He even went as far as to offer the staff at Shepperton a 50 per cent share in the studio if they dropped their opposition to his redevelopment plans for forty acres of the site.

But in the midst of these negotiations, Bentley found himself ousted when he became the victim of yet another hostile takeover, as his own Barclay Securities was bought out for some £18.5 million by the J. H. Vavasseur Group. It was eventually

Nicolas Roeg directs David Bowie at his most alienated as Thomas Newton Jerome in 1976's *The Man Who Fell to Earth*. Co-star Candy Clark looks on, at Shepperton Studios.

decided that three of the stages would be taken down and that land would be sold for housing. The studio would remain on a twenty-two-acre site, with the promise of no redundancies, ensuring that Shepperton would continue to be a viable competitor to rival Pinewood.

The sense of relief was, however, short-lived. The continued downturn in UK film production meant that by the following year, 1974, it was decided that Shepperton would become a facility for hire, with productions bringing in their own crews and many of the studio's employees losing their jobs after all.

In September of that year, the studio's assets were further stripped and a five-day auction was held to sell off equipment, props, costumes and more. It was a low point for the once-glorious studio that Alexander Korda had helped to build.

'I walked around the whole studio on my own, through the set of *Oliver!*, everywhere. I walked into editing rooms, and all the doors were unlocked. It was my studio. Then I walked out through the front gate, past the guards.'

Newly arrived in the UK, Terry Gilliam breaks into Shepperton

Productions were still coming to Shepperton, but they were few and far between. Hollywood legend John Wayne brought his tough US cop *Brannigan* to London and based production at Shepperton, whilst Nicolas Roeg cast the other-worldly pop star David Bowie as the other-worldly *Man Who Fell to Earth*, also based at the studio. Gregory Peck was shipped in from Tinseltown to star in director Richard Donner's occult classic *The Omen*, which became one of the largest box office successes of the mid 1970s.

Meanwhile, a little science fiction film called *Star Wars* briefly moved on to H Stage but was, for the most part, based out at Elstree.

Many years earlier, on his arrival to England from his native America, nascent film-maker and soon-to-be Python Terry Gilliam broke into Shepperton Studios. He was visiting nearby Hampton Court and popped over to the studio. When the guards on the gate refused him entry, an undeterred Gilliam went around the corner, climbed over the wall and proceeded to make himself at home for the day.

'I walked around the whole studio on my own,' he recalls, 'through the set of *Oliver!*, everywhere. I walked into editing rooms, and all the doors were unlocked. It was my studio. Then I walked out through the front gate, past the guards. Years later, I made *Jabberwocky* there.'

In 1976, the year of lowest production in Shepperton's history to that point, Gilliam found his solo directorial debut one of the few films being made at the once busy studio. He even ended up re-dressing the street set from *Oliver!* that he had walked around so freely all those years before.

Having just come off the success of *Monty Python and the Holy Grail*, with *Jabberwocky* he was once again back in medieval times, even if he couldn't afford to bring his vision fully to life at the studio.

'I miss the camaraderie of the crews, and, in particular, being on set every day with Cubby Broccoli.

Roger Moore retires his 007

'We had no money,' he recalls. 'So for the big sets we hired some rubber flagstones, but we could only hire a few, so we'd put them down on the floor and just light those areas. For the walls we managed to get enough rubber and plaster stones to go up to about eight feet. The rest is black drapes. People thought there were Python millions after *Holy Grail*, and that *Jabberwocky* should be a big film. There'd be a moment like where Bernard Bresslaw was getting out of jail, and we didn't have a set. We had a door, some bars and one of our windows. And the crew was screaming, "But this is not a set!" and I said, "I don't need a set. I need a window, blackness, and some bars, and you see his face and hand come through and that's all you need. It tells a story." It's really hard to get some people to think like that.'

Shortly after taking over British Lion and Shepperton, following the coup that said goodbye to John Bentley and his company, new studio chairman Barry Spikings and managing director Michael Deeley struck a deal to partner with EMI (who had already taken charge of MGM's Borehamwood lot). But still the future of Shepperton was up in the air. The recent changes of ownership were not to be the end of it. Harry Saltzman, who had recently parted ways with his long-time Bond partner Cubby Broccoli, had relocated from Pinewood to Shepperton – and decided he liked the company so much he wanted to buy it.

Saltzman put in a bid for the whole studios at £8 million. But by then the deal to sell off a significant amount of the land for housing was in place, and so Saltzman's offer – which would have seen the studio remain in its original form – was rejected. Pinewood was still attracting productions on the scale of the US dystopian science fiction drama *Rollerball*, starring James Caan, and soon-to-be world-beating film-

The film that wasn't the sequel to *Monty Python and the Holy Grail* (despite what Eric Idle's home-made T-shirt says here). Having once scaled the fence and broken into Shepperton Studios, Terry Gilliam returned there in 1976 to make his solo directing debut with *Jabberwocky*. Naturally, despite hiding in a barrel, he got a helping hand from a few friends – Terry Jones, Michael Palin and Eric Idle.

makers such as Alan Parker, whose children-led gangster musical *Bugsy Malone* took over the studio's stages for a while before Parker moved in himself, basing his Alan Parker Film Company at Pinewood for the next ten years.

But overall film production in the UK was slow, with the studio forced to rely more and more on television. The classic 1960s spy show *The Avengers*, for example, was revamped as *The New Avengers* and added Joanna Lumley and Gareth Hunt as new sidekicks to Patrick Macnee's veteran John Steed.

Gerry Anderson also returned to the studio. Having shot his first live-action series, *UFO*, there in the early '70s, he now tackled his most ambitious project, *Space 1999*. Sold in part as a British *Star Trek*, *Space 1999* brought in the high-profile casting of American husband and wife (and former *Mission: Impossible* stars) Martin Landau and Barbara Bain. It also saw the return of FX (special effects) veteran Brian Johnson.

The model work that Johnson had done on *Thunderbirds*, *2001: A Space Odyssey* and more had clearly had an impact on younger film-makers around the world, and when *Space 1999* was renewed for a second season, Johnson found himself having to turn down a job with one of those young film-makers, shooting a new project in London.

'Some people from 20th Century Fox came down and said, "We're gonna be doing this science fiction movie and we'd be interested in you being involved." I'd just signed with Gerry Anderson to do a second series of Space 1999. It was George Lucas.'

Brian Johnson on lost opportunities

'Some people from 20th Century Fox came down to see the work we were doing and said, "We're gonna be doing this science fiction movie and we'd be interested in you being involved doing the models and stuff." I said, "Yeah, okay. When is this to be?" And he mentioned the time and I said, "Well, that's not possible because I've just signed with Gerry Anderson to do a second series of *Space 1999*." One of the guys said, "Well, that's all right, we intend to do a series of these things and we'll get you for the second one." Then they had a look at what I was doing with the camera and multiple exposures and everything else and asked why we weren't using motion controls. I said, "Because I've got to do six shots a day." Then one of them said, "Well, we'll be back in touch with you." It was George Lucas. He and Gary Kurtz had come round to have a look and see what was going on.'

TV production continued at Pinewood when the classic '60s spy show was revived as *The New Avengers*. Here we see Joanna Lumley, Gareth Hunt and Patrick Macnee, returning as John Steed, armed and dangerous in the Pinewood gardens, 1976.

Alan Parker made his mark – and a helluva mess – as his debut *Bugsy Malone* splurged its way across Pinewood in 1976.

Johnson may well have missed out on *Star Wars* due to his prior commitment to Anderson's TV show, but, true to their word, Lucas and Kurtz did come calling for their second movie, *The Empire Strikes Back* – for which Johnson won an Academy Award. Despite such active TV production, in 1975 Pinewood had posted a loss of £450,000, and with the high taxation system in the UK, the studio was finding itself increasingly unable to lure foreign projects to the country, losing scheduled productions such as *Equus* to places like Canada. The studio was forced to lay off much of its workforce, reducing staff from over 1,300 to around 700, leading to talk of the Rank Organisation even selling off the studios completely.

Rather than taking that drastic step, the new chairman of Rank, Ed Chilton, announced that the company was going back into financing film production. The first result of this endeavour, the lamentable big-screen Wombles outing *Wombling Free*, was a major disaster, barely securing a release, and merely adding to Pinewood's financial troubles.

Similarly, the once world-beating facilities that Korda had sought to create at Shepperton were in disarray, whilst Pinewood, despite having just built the world's largest stage, was about to lose its biggest tenant. The two studios were at the lowest point in their once illustrious lives.

Only a Superman could save them.

Thankfully, there was one about to move in.

Gerry Anderson brought his latest science fiction series to Pinewood in 1975. Imported American star Martin Landau gets his hand made up for an episode of *Space 1999*.

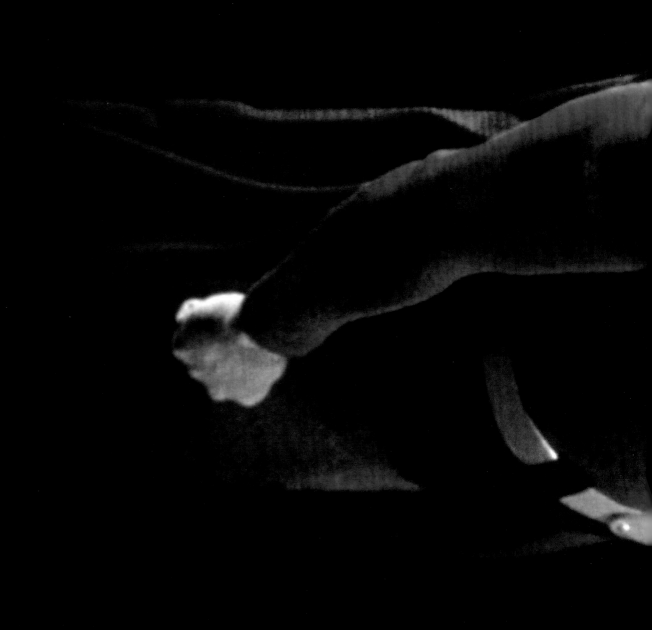

LOOK, UP
IN THE SKY

N O ONE REALLY KNEW IT YET, but the film world was about to change. A little-known and relatively low-budget space movie called *Star Wars* shot in the UK in 1976, largely at Elstree, with some extra work at Shepperton. Upon its release in May of 1977, *Star Wars* would almost single-handedly revolutionise the world of cinema, ushering in the era of the modern blockbuster, the summer movie, with ever-wider release patterns matched by increasing budgets and, potentially, huge profits.

Although *Star Wars* had yet to open and establish this subsequent pervading paradigm, Alexander and Ilya Salkind's planned production of *Superman* was a film conceived in that image.

Brought to life in 1938 on the pages of the first issue of *Action Comics* by creators Jerry Siegel and Joe Shuster, Superman remained a hugely popular figure over the following decades, although his screen appearances (cartoons aside) were confined to a creaky big-screen serial in the 1940s, and a much more successful TV show in the 1950s. But a big-screen feature film had never happened, something the Salkinds, alongside co-producer Pierre Spengler, set out to rectify in 1974.

Two years of pre-production saw the movie briefly set up to shoot in Rome, with Bond director Guy Hamilton on board, before logistics found it relocating to the UK and finding a home initially at Shepperton. Hamilton, however, couldn't work in the UK on what was to be a lengthy production due to the country's prohibitive tax system, so he was forced to bow out. The Salkinds replaced him with veteran American director Richard Donner, who had been busy over at Shepperton filming what was shortly to become a major hit for him, the Gregory Peck-starring son-of-Satan movie *The Omen*.

With Hamilton's late departure, Donner came on board only eleven weeks before shooting was scheduled to begin. 'I got a call one day from a European voice,' Donner later recalled, 'that said, "This is Alexander Salkind. You know who I am?" And I said, "No." And he said, "I produced *The Three Musketeers*. We're doing *Superman* now, and we just saw *The Omen*, would you like to do it?" So I said, "That's flattering, but I'd like to read it first." And his reaction was "You don't have to read it. Everybody likes it." But I said, "Well, I'd feel better if I read it."'

Despite Salkind calling from Europe and Donner being based in California, a script arrived with the director a mere twenty minutes later.

In 1978 Superman moved in as James Bond moved out of the newly constructed 007 Stage, replacing *The Spy Who Loved Me*'s nuclear submarine pen, with Superman's Fortress of Solitude.

PRECEDING PAGE: You'll believe a man can fly. Christopher Reeve dons the famous red cape for 1978's *Superman: The Movie*.

'Literally, that's how fast it was here. I called him back and said that I would be interested if I could do a major rewrite and bring in a new writer. But they said they were very happy with the screenplay and everybody liked it; so I said, "We had better forget about it." Meanwhile, though, they were negotiating with my agent, and my agent called and said, "Boy, have I got you a deal." I told him I didn't want it. Anyway, it went on hassling back and forth, and finally they agreed. So I flew over to Paris and made the deal.'

'You had European producers and a British director making an American fable. And nothing wrong with it, except I don't think they knew what the fable was.'

Richard Donner comes on board to sort out *Superman*

Donner was offered the not inconsiderable sum of $1 million to come on board. The script he had read was a whopping 550-page shooting script – 'And they planned to shoot all 550 pages. You know 110 pages is plenty for a script.' He later described the state of the production that Guy Hamilton had developed with the Salkinds. 'You had European producers and a British director making an American fable. And nothing was wrong with it, except I don't think they knew what the fable was.'

Alongside the script, the Salkinds had also sent Donner a Superman costume. 'I got a little stoned, smoked some weed, put on the Superman costume. I was in pretty good shape then. It was like elastic.'

Once out of costume, Donner quickly set about supervising a complete rewrite, by noted screenwriter Tom Mankiewicz, alongside scouting locations and, of course, finding his Superman.

As pre-production was rolling on, the producers proved themselves adept at drumming up publicity for their big-budget movie, especially when it came to the casting of the iconic son of Krypton. The likes of Robert Redford, Warren Beatty, Clint Eastwood, Kris Kristofferson and Burt Reynolds all talked or tested. Dustin Hoffman passed on both that role and that of Superman's nemesis Lex Luthor, whilst recent Olympic-gold-medal-winning athlete Bruce Jenner (now known as Caitlyn Jenner) went in for an unsuccessful screen test.

In a 2016 piece Donner wrote for the *Hollywood Reporter*, he recalled that even recent *Rocky*'s Sylvester Stallone was in the running. 'The Salkinds wanted a name. I met with Sylvester Stallone because of them. I tried to be nice and said, "This is wrong." I liked Stallone; he turned out to be a nice guy. He wanted to do it. He was a

Christopher Reeve pays attention to his director Donner whilst filming *Superman: The Movie* (1978).

big star and I'm some punk kid. A lot of actors wanted to do it. They gave me a list of all these names and I said, "Listen. Your flying stuff is shit, and I have to create a man who flies. Even if you saw Paul Newman or Robert Redford in that costume, no one is going to believe them." I fought for an unknown.'

In the end, Donner and the Salkinds unveiled the relatively unknown Christopher Reeve as the Man of Steel, even though Donner was initially unsure, citing both the actor's youth and lack of bulk. 'One of the actors comes in and it's this kid, Chris Reeve,' he wrote in the *Hollywood Reporter*. 'He walks in; he's got this great big sweater on, blondish hair. I said, "What's under the sweater?" and he says, "Well …" I said, "Problem quite honestly, buster, is I got to get a guy that is bulk, that looks like a muscle zoo." He said, "Listen, I was a jock in school and when I went into acting I lost fifty pounds." I said, "I don't believe you, you're an actor." He says, "No, I did. I swear to you."

'I went to see him in a play that night. It was some off-Broadway thing. He played two roles, as a son and a grandfather. And I kind of hired him on faith. I had to go back to London and I flew Chris back, which was so far from his life. When he told his father, who was a professor at Princeton, that he was doing *Superman*, his father said, "*Man and Superman*?" (referring to the George Bernard Shaw play).'

Eager to ensure their film was not riding on the shoulders of such a novice, box office star (and, ironically, Dustin Hoffman's former roommate) Gene Hackman was cast as arch-villain Lex Luthor.

'When he told his father, who was a professor at Princeton, that he was doing *Superman*, his father said, "*Man and Superman*?"'
Christopher Reeve tries not to disappoint his parents with his big casting news

But the Salkinds' real casting coup came in the form of Superman's father, Jor-El. After a few years in his own artistic wilderness, Marlon Brando had burst back on to the screen and was by now one of the most high-profile movie stars of the 1970s, following the huge success of both *The Godfather* and *Last Tango in Paris*. The producers signed him for what was little more than a cameo (albeit a cameo with top billing), but despite the brevity of the part, Brando secured headlines worldwide and upped the expectations of this comic-book movie, especially when they paid him what was then the biggest salary in movie history – $3.7 million for just twelve days' shooting and what amounted to just a few minutes of screen time.

Donner later said of the casting, 'They didn't hire Marlon Brando the actor; they hired Marlon Brando the name.'

The first scenes Donner shot on the movie were with Brando (who introduced himself to the director by suggesting, 'You know, maybe I shouldn't look like people on Krypton. Maybe I should look like a bagel'), mere weeks after he'd come aboard, weeks that were very busy for the director. 'I went to work on the picture the first week in January 1977 and eleven weeks later we were shooting with Brando. They had prepared the picture for a year, but not one bit of it was useful to me. I brought in a new writer, Tom Mankiewicz, and a new art director, John Barry, and we started from scratch.

'Maybe I shouldn't look like people on Krypton. Maybe I should look like a bagel?'

Marlon Brando took the role of Jor-El very seriously

'Tom was with me every second in London,' Donner recalled. 'Every morning my driver picked him up – I had a driver under contract, seven days a week, twenty-four hours, whenever I needed him. Every day, I had them pick up Tom, then we would drive to Pinewood or Shepperton. We shot at both.'

Shooting with Brando created some problems, rather than learning his lines, he had taken to reading them from cards carefully concealed around the set. 'He was totally present, on time. Not difficult,' Donner says. 'We had to put his dialogue on other actors' chests. He would say, "I don't want to read like I've read it before a bunch of times. The first time I read it, it'll be honest." He made it work. He was the ultimate. He was Marlon Brando. He was Marlon fucking Brando.'

At this time, the Salkinds were riding high on the success of their all-star take on *The Three Musketeers* and *The Four Musketeers*, both of which had been directed by Richard Lester. They had shot the two movies back to back, partly to save money on production, but also to help reduce the salaries of the cast. With *Superman* planned as the first of a series, they decided to adopt the same approach here and attempt to shoot two for the price of one.

Production on what was now called *Superman: The Movie* began on 28 March 1977 at Shepperton, but Donner and Co. began to fall behind schedule right from the off, and it soon became apparent just how big this production was. Shepperton was quickly deemed too small and ill-equipped to accommodate the film's needs, so a decision was made to relocate to Pinewood, where the newly built 007 Stage, recently vacated by *The Spy Who Loved Me*'s subs, was taken over by Superman's ice-bound Fortress of Solitude.

'I had a golf cart with a radio in it,' Donner told *Cinefantastique* magazine, recalling

Cinematographer Geoffrey Unswoth, brings Krypton to life before Kal-El begins the journey that will bring him to Earth. Unsworth, a two-time Oscar winner for *Cabaret* and *Tess*, sadly died before the release of *Superman: The Movie*. The film is dedicated to him.

the frantic nature of the production, 'and my office would have the home base radio. And I'd get calls all over the lot: "You're wanted on A Stage for a line-up … the 007 Stage is ready for a rehearsal … you're needed in the cutting room …" So, I'd just travel from one to the other. It was bananas. But I had to be in every one of those places because it was all in my head.'

Superman's arrival was, in many ways, the lifeline Pinewood desperately needed at this time. With film production at an all-time low, the studio was in serious financial straits. Pinewood had earlier been forced to turn the *Superman* production away, since Bond was still shooting. But after the subsequent delays in production, the studio was now in a position to accommodate the Salkinds. Thus, Superman not only saved the world, but Pinewood Studios as well.

Still, the production itself was falling further and further behind schedule, with Donner's relationship with on-set producer Pierre Spengler worsening on a daily basis, and rumours flying that the producers were increasingly dissatisfied with the director and planning to replace him. This rumour was given some credence when they brought their *Musketeers* director Richard Lester on board as producer.

As Donner recently recalled of this difficult period, 'The producers kept saying, "You're going over budget." And I would say, "How am I going over budget if I don't know what the budget is?"'

The film's poster would eventually bear the legend 'You'll Believe a Man Can Fly', and one of the main reasons for delay on the film was the numerous attempts to make that happen. Donner and his team tried many methods to achieve the effect, from a brief attempt at skydiving to dangling a stuntman from a crane.

'They kept saying, "You're going over budget." And I would say, "How am I going over budget if I don't know what the budget is?"'

Richard Donner

'We tried flying a stuntman from a 300-foot crane behind the Golden Gate Bridge miniature,' said Donner. 'And since the bridge was only about sixty feet long, we tried to have him behind the model several hundred feet, and we'd swing him from this monstrous crane in a long sweeping arc. That didn't work.'

Eventually effects cameraman Zoran Perisic invented a unique new form of front projection that essentially meant that Christopher Reeve could be filmed in the air but not actually in motion as the background and camera swooped and moved around him, creating the illusion of flight.

Marlon Brando clowns around with producer Alexander Salkind on the set of *Superman: The Movie*.

You'll believe a man can cry. A clownish Roger Moore refused to see the funny side when *Superman* star Christopher Reeve showed up on the set of *Octopussy* (1983) at Pinewood.

If the flying proved problematic for Donner, the cape was nearly as bad. Superman's cape, an integral part of the hero's costume, simply wouldn't cooperate when flying. It just didn't look like that was what it was doing. Or, as Donner more succinctly put it, 'That cape was a bitch!' Over fifty capes were made, of different weights and lengths, some with wire frameworks that could be manipulated by hidden gears, and bottled air was blown at them, until eventually Donner had the effect he wanted. Then the director found himself redesigning Superman's boots, as the producers had not originally realised that they would be filmed from varying angles. 'Those sort of things were so easily anticipated,' the director said, 'but nobody did it.'

Special effects supervisor Derek Meddings, meanwhile, was busy taking over other parts of Pinewood to bring the rest of the film's visuals to life. As well as building a sixty-foot version of the Golden Gate Bridge on the backlot, Meddings and his team filled F Stage with a model of the planet Krypton, suspended twenty feet off the ground, and eventually blew it up spectacularly. The model master also used the exterior Paddock Tank to build another large-scale model, this time of the Boulder Dam, which was required to burst. 'What we did was to get about six huge water pumps,' Meddings explained to *American Cinematographer*, 'and we pumped the water from the paddock tank up to the level of the dam, then we constructed a platform made of aluminium, so that when the dam burst, the water pumped over the edge. It continued to pump a huge volume of water without the level dropping – which meant that we could hold the shot for long enough to show the water bursting through the dam and flooding the valley below.'

Superman: The Movie was released in 1978 and proved to be a massive box office success. Production on *Superman II* continued at Pinewood, but by now Richard Donner, despite having already shot a large part of the sequel, had departed the production. 'I got a call from my agent, who said, "I just received a telegram from the Salkinds. You are no longer needed." That was it.

'These two years took everything out of me – *everything*. It even took the enjoyment out of film-making. It was a very trying time.'

Richard Lester was already on hand and happy to take over the reins. The first sequel saw the Pinewood backlot converted into a full-scale American street for the final battle between Superman and Terence Stamp's General Zod, complete with upturned buses, crushed taxis and exploding tankers.

The Salkinds brought the production of *Superman III* back to the studio in 1982, and a spin-off production in the form of Kal-El's cousin *Supergirl* in 1983. Despite the financial benefits these ongoing shows brought to Pinewood in otherwise lean times, the series became one of diminishing returns, losing its appeal at the box office, and was halted after 1987's misguided *Superman IV: The Quest for Peace*.

FOLLOWING PAGE: The backlot at Pinewood was converted into a classic slice of small-town American life for *Supergirl* (1984), at the time one of the largest exterior sets built at the studio. 'To make it look as if it went on longer we built the end part of the street in perspective, and that was raised up to about eight feet high,' recalls the film's supervising art director Terry Ackland-Snow. 'In those days people used to take their families to look at the set and one guy drove along it and then he sped off the end of it. He thought it was getting smaller and then the next minute he's dropped eight feet.'

SHEPPERTON GETS AN ALIEN OF THEIR OWN

I N 1977, BRITISH LION CEASED TRADING. EMI moved in and bought their prestigious film library, and The Who moved in and bought a large part of Shepperton. Their Rampart Company paid £350,000 for a ninety-nine-year lease on the old house, and the band quickly set themselves up as lords of the manor, also making use of J and K stages, which they used for rehearsals and filming.

A large percentage of the money The Who had paid was ploughed into upgrading the studio, and into this refurbished environment in 1978 came Ridley Scott.

The Royal College of Art graduate director had previously been working – very successfully – in advertising.

'The first commercial I ever directed was with Peter Sims and company for Regent Petrol from the agency Young & Rubicam,' he recalls fondly of his early career. 'This would be my debut into advertising – a pretty girl in a cowboy hat, who would blow on the end of the petrol pump as if it were a gun! I was into it for life!'

He went on to shoot many commercials at both Pinewood and Shepperton in what was to turn out to be a golden era in British advertising.

'From the outset it was always a serious creative process for me. I would only think of commercials as small vignettes of feature films. Which is why I was so successful and constantly busy for the next thirty years. First came small studios in Soho. Then Knightly, Isleworth. Finally the big jobs. I shot at least fifteen years of my thirty-year career at Pinewood and Shepperton. I like the studio atmosphere, the old stages, with all their incredible history: Orson Welles ... Michael Powell ... David Lean ... Carol Reed.

'It was the heyday of British advertising,' he continues. 'New – very competitive, very creative and extraordinarily exciting. We were the best in the business and joining me were Adrian Lyne, Alan Parker, Hugh Hudson, my brother Tony Scott, Paul Ibbetson. This was truly a terrific creative breeding ground for new talent to evolve and compete with the best in the world.'

But as satisfying as Scott found the advertising world, he had always wanted to make features.

'My first film did not occur until 1977,' he says. '*The Duellists* was all shot on location, was well received, and it opened the door to Hollywood.'

Now, inspired in part by *2001: A Space Odyssey* (which had shot at the studio a decade before) and the recent game-changing impact of *Star Wars*, Scott moved into Shepperton to make *Alien*. The film was one of the biggest productions the studio had seen in years, making Scott something of a saviour, a role he would perform once again when he and his brother, and their backers, came to buy Shepperton several years later.

'I was offered *Alien*, with an $8.2 million budget, and I was able to make it in England,' recalls Scott of his second movie as director. 'I knew I was so much more at ease working at UK studios, providing so many skills. And I already knew all the crew members, carpenters, riggers, etc. I must have shot on H Stage at least a hundred times before I built the *Alien* landscape there.'

A young Ridley Scott gets behind the camera for his second feature, *Alien*.

PRECEDING PAGE: Ridley Scott and his team took inspiration from the work of Swiss surrealist artist H. R. Giger and, in particular, his book *Necronomicon* in designing their xenomorph for 1979's *Alien*.

The movie was written by Dan O'Bannon and Ronald Shusett. Earlier in the decade O'Bannon had worked as both writer and actor on John Carpenter's debut, *Dark Star*, an almost comic take on the movie Scott would come to make, with what was essentially a beach ball with claw feet standing in for the alien. Originally known as *Star Beast*, *Alien* would very much prove to be the dark side of *Dark Star*. By the time Scott came across the script, it had already been through the hands of producers Walter Hill and David Giler.

'I already knew all the crew members, carpenters, riggers, etc. I must have shot on H Stage at least a hundred times before I built the *Alien* landscape there.'

Ridley Scott on being at home at Shepperton

'I was shown the reworked Dan O'Bannon script and at the time I was at a standstill with *Tristan and Isolde*, an Arthurian tale about knights and sorcery,' Scott recalled at the time, referring to the movie he had planned to follow *The Duellists* with. 'So I was looking for something really special. I was immediately attracted to *Alien* for the same reason I was attracted to Joseph Conrad's *The Duellists*. It was so simple, so linear, so pure, an idea with no fat. The script was short and very specific – and unbelievably violent. It took me less than forty-five minutes to read. That really impressed me. I sensed that it would play even faster than it read.'

For the sophomore director it meant not only stepping into a new genre, science fiction – '*2001: A Space Odyssey* was my personal revelation and I began to speculate on what could be done in space. Then came *Star Wars* and *Close Encounters of the Third Kind*, and I recognised the tremendous quality that was possible in making these films stand head and shoulders above the usual quickie space flick … I saw something utterly different and compelling in *Alien*' – but also exploring the way that *Alien* offered the chance to make a horror movie in a traditional science fiction environment. 'In the few horror movies that I'd seen, with the exception of one or two, the creatures hadn't been good. As soon as you accept a script like this, you begin to worry about what you're going to do with "the man in the rubber suit". So the alien became our first priority. We had to make it totally repulsive and yet scary as hell. I looked at sketches of blobs and octopuses and dinosaurs. They were all awful.'

2001: A Space Odyssey veteran Brian Johnson was recruited to build models for Scott's film, and can attest that the film-maker did a lot more than just look at sketches; he was making most of them himself.

'Ridley was seriously hands-on, he'd done these fantastic sketches and storyboards,' Johnson recalls. 'He was more on the ball than probably anyone I'd ever worked with. And the script was great. Bray Studios was where I based myself. But then we moved out to Shepperton to do the effects on *Alien*.'

O'Bannon, meanwhile, was on hand to help Ridley with his burgeoning horror education. 'Before he started working on *Alien*, he sat down on my recommendation and watched *The Texas Chainsaw Massacre*,' the writer recalled to *Cinefantastique* magazine. 'And he came out ecstatic; he loved it. And it surprised me because Ridley's films are so lush and romantic. He made *everybody* watch *The Texas Chainsaw Massacre*, which is documentary and stark and violent.'

Scott himself elaborated on this to the same magazine, shortly after *Alien*'s release. 'I happen to be a great admirer of Tobe Hooper's *The Texas Chainsaw Massacre*. That film was absolutely, utterly relentless – a real heart-stopper. But Hooper overdid it. If he had just eased back a bit, if he had let you off the hook a couple of times, he could have captured a much broader audience.'

With Shepperton Studios booked in to shoot the movie, Scott and his team had four months of pre-production before shooting began on 25 July 1978. During that time, the director had to solve the problem of 'the man in the rubber suit'. He went some way to addressing this issue when he came across a book of artwork by Swiss surrealist painter H. R. Giger. It was in the pages of Giger's *Necronomicon* that Scott found the design for his own star beast. 'It was the most frightening thing I'd ever seen,' the director recalled. 'I knew immediately that here was our creature.'

'Ridley was seriously hands-on, he'd done these fantastic sketches and storyboards. He was more on the ball than probably anyone I'd ever worked with.'

Brian Johnson comes on board to provide *Alien* with its Oscar-winning FX

Scott was hugely impressed with Giger's work and its biomechanical nature, so much so that he flew the artist over to England and had him ensconced at Shepperton. 'I brought H. R. Giger in from Switzerland and gave him one of the small stages as his private workshop. I would enter every afternoon to discuss and look at the progress of the alien in all its forms – egg, face hugger, fully grown xenomorph, etc. Giger also worked on the ship and the landscape.'

Giger did indeed contribute significantly to the design of the crashed spacecraft first encountered by the crew of the *Nostromo*. Realised on an enormous set at

Ridley Scott introduces a partly costumed John Hurt to Giger's Space Jockey on H Stage at Shepperton during filming for *Alien* (1979).

Shepperton and featuring a Giger-designed creature that became known as the Space Jockey, this construction initially created a few problems for the production designer Michael Seymour. Lacking the budget to build the derelict spaceship to Giger's specifications, Seymour came up with the idea of placing the Space Jockey on a turntable at the centre of the set, allowing Scott to shoot from seemingly different angles and giving the impression of a fully enclosed set. (The lasers used at the beginning of this sequence, as the crew enter the downed ship, were provided by Shepperton residents The Who, who were using them to rehearse a new live show on the sound stage next to Scott and his doomed astronauts.)

'It was the most frightening thing I'd ever seen. I knew immediately that here was our creature.'

Scott finds inspiration in the work of Swiss surrealist H. R. Giger

Design by H. R. Giger, direction by Scott – *Alien* blasts off at Shepperton.

Giger may well have designed the alien, but Scott turned to FX expert Carlo Rambaldi to build the perfect terrifying beast. To avoid the whole issue of 'the man in the rubber suit', Scott had decided to largely avoid showing the suit (which would be worn by six-foot-ten-inch Bolaji Badejo). Instead, he relied on Rambaldi to bring Giger's extended dark and smooth phallic head – complete with teeth-encrusted tongue – to life. The FX master had recently been responsible for creating part of a life-size King Kong for producer Dino De Laurentiis and the alien figures for Steven Spielberg in *Close Encounters of the Third Kind*. 'I got a call from the *Alien* production office in London,' he explained to *Cinefantastique* at the time, 'because it was impossible for them to get what they wanted over there.' Rambaldi studied Giger's designs and signed up, promising to deliver Scott his alien in four weeks.

Rambaldi soon decamped to Shepperton to join the production, where he constructed three heads for the creature, each with different functions, from curling its lips, to shooting its tongue through the heads of unsuspecting crew members, to dripping saliva though its hungry jaws – in reality, the ever-reliable KY Jelly. During filming, up to six members of the creature builder's team were responsible for operating these complex movements at any one time, and as Rambaldi pointed out, 'The head's profile banishes any thought of a man in a suit.'

Brian Johnson and his team, who had been responsible for building and filming the intricate models the shoot required, were also brought in to cover up the workings of Rambaldi's complex mechanisms.

'Carlo Rambaldi built the alien,' says Johnson, 'but when it got on the set there were all these springs everywhere sticking out. He didn't have the facilities over here so my boys rearranged everything so the springs weren't sticking out. And they got Bolaji Badejo to wear it. God knows how tall he was, but he spent quite a lot of the

time in that suit. He used to pass out from the heat.'

For all their troubles, Rambaldi, Giger and Johnson were rewarded with that year's Oscar for Best Visual Effects, alongside Nick Allder and Dennis Ayling.

Despite the obvious success of the creature – in both design and execution – Rambaldi remained somewhat disappointed by the way Scott chose to hide the alien, keeping its form a fixture of shadow and uncertainty. 'I would have preferred more screen time for the audience to notice details,' he once recounted. 'In my opinion I gave the director a hundred possibilities, and he used about twenty. Perhaps he had a reason for this approach. Perhaps he thought the alien was better left to the imagination.'

As on the ball as Scott was, he still was hesitant in committing to a creature that wasn't absolutely what he had inside his head, as Brian Johnson also observed when it came to the building of the film's ship, the *Nostromo*. 'Ridley couldn't make up his mind what he wanted. When we got to the *Nostromo* he kept changing things. I said, "I want to build a small model. I'll bring the model to you and you can look at it. If you want to change things we can always sort it at that stage but I don't want to do it with an eighteen-foot-long model. It would be too late to change." So I brought this thing over and he kept adding bits and pieces here and there, but basically he liked it. So I said, "Okay, lads, I'll sit down and build it full scale," and then Ridley changed his mind again. So we had to actually chop bits off and add bits here, there and everywhere. But we got it done in the end with a million bits of plastic kit on the outside.'

Back on the floor at Shepperton, Scott had opted to design the full-size version of that spaceship as a worn and lived-in environment, full of rubbish and edged with rust. More significantly, he designed all the sections of the ship to be built as fully enclosed four-walled and ceilinged sets, increasing the claustrophobic feel of the environment, ramping up the tension for both the audience and the actors, who had never worked in such a manner before.

And of course, Scott, Giger and Co. had a few tricks up their sleeves – again, for audience and cast alike – with more than one iteration of the alien being revealed. John Hurt found himself in close proximity to one of them when the FX team rigged him to have the now infamous chest-burster version of the alien explode from his shirt – much to the surprise of the blood-soaked cast around him, who had not been warned what to expect in advance.

Hurt himself coped well with having his chest explode on set. 'He had to have a chilled bottle of wine waiting for him,' Brian Johnson recalls. 'One of my boys supplied it.'

Creating a new kind of screen heroine – Ridley Scott instructs Sigourney Weaver on her first time in space in *Alien* (1979).

FOLLOWING PAGES: Thirty-three years after he first journeyed to LV-426, Sir Ridley Scott returned to his *Alien* world, this time with Noomi Rapace as his latest female icon for the 2012 prequel *Prometheus*.

Alien shot for sixteen weeks at Shepperton, where Scott remained to finish editing and effects work. 'There's nothing supremely intellectual about *Alien*,' he said shortly afterwards. 'That's the point of the film. It has absolutely no message. It works on a very visceral level and its only point is terror, and more terror.'

No argument here. On its release in the summer of 1979, it became a huge hit – making a star out of Sigourney Weaver – and remains a seminal film in not one but two genres, having redefined both the science fiction movie and the horror film – a veritable haunted house movie in space.

'There's nothing supremely intellectual about *Alien*. That's the point of the film. It has absolutely no message. It works on a very visceral level and its only point is terror, and more terror.'

Scott on his science fiction/horror mash-up masterpiece

Ridley Scott behind the camera on *Alien* at Shepperton Studios in 1979; 16 years later he and his brother Tony would buy the studio.

FOLLOWING PAGE: When you find yourself in need of a laser or two, just pop next door and ask the neighbours – Scott made use of Shepperton resident's The Who's stage kit to light up his alien world.

Scott also said at the time of *Alien*'s release, 'My next film will certainly not be science fiction.' His next film turned out to be *Blade Runner*, probably one of the most influential science fiction films in the history of cinema.

In 1980, EMI merged with electrical company Thorn, becoming Thorn EMI, and announced they were abandoning investment in film production. Another major blow for the declining British film industry.

Production did continue, however – even if Shepperton only played host to a single film shoot in the wake of *Alien*. *Flash Gordon* was produced by Italian movie mogul Dino De Laurentiis, and was another movie aiming to ride the coat-tails of a post-*Star Wars* universe. Nicolas Roeg, fresh from his own extraterrestrial musings with *The Man Who Fell to Earth*, was originally slated to direct, but passed on the project. Mike Hodges stepped in, later admitting that he was saddled with an extensive art department that spoke only Italian – which he himself didn't – and so found himself literally making it up as he went along.

The film, with an accompanying score by rock band Queen, initially flopped on its release a year later, but went on to develop a sizeable cult following over the years.

BUILDING CHARACTER

PINEWOOD BEGAN THE NEW DECADE with an absence of Bond, a reliance on Superman and the return of Sean Connery. The latter was cast as the lead in Peter Hyams' western-like space drama *Outland* (often described as '*High Noon* in space' – for the very good reason that its plot is almost identical).

At the same time the studio was playing home to a western very clearly not set in space. Hot from the Oscar-winning success of his *The Deer Hunter* the year before, director Michael Cimino embarked on his epic western *Heaven's Gate*, a film that went so over budget and proved so disastrous on release that it led to the demise of United Artists, a company whose UK production office had only recently relocated to the main hall at Pinewood.

With fewer and fewer productions moving on to the lot, one, at least, made good use of the studio and its environs. Inspired by the 1980 Iranian Embassy siege in London, and its successful resolution by the SAS, *Who Dares Wins* was a take on the Special Armed Services – led by popular *Professionals* actor Lewis Collins – and a terrorist takeover of the US Embassy. Richard Widmark played the US ambassador, alongside a then-emerging Judy Davis as the leader of the terrorists.

Pinewood's own restaurant doubled for the ambassador's lavishly appointed dining room, whilst the exterior of Heatherden Hall stood in for the embassy itself, complete with an extra floor added by production designer Syd Cain. For several days the quiet, leafy grounds around Pinewood's central building were assaulted by the droning of helicopters and the abseiling of stuntmen down the front of the studio's offices.

Mel Brooks, who by 1980 was past his glory days as a comedy film-maker, briefly moved into Shepperton for his uneven comedy *History of the World, Part I*, in which he starred alongside such Brooks regulars as Madeline Kahn, Harvey Korman, Dom DeLuise and Cloris Leachman, as well as newcomers to the world of Brooks, Gregory Hines, Pamela Stephenson and Orson Welles.

More significantly, as producer under his Brooksfilms shingle, Brooks brought a young film-maker named David Lynch to Shepperton. Brooks had seen Lynch's cult late-night industrial nightmare of a movie *Eraserhead*, declared Lynch 'a madman' and started to consider the director for his next project, *The Elephant Man*. This was the true-life story of Joseph (John) Merrick, the deformed circus performer of the title, liberated from his existence by a prominent surgeon of the day, who, fascinated by his physical condition, turned him into something of a society figure in Victorian London.

1982's *Who Dares Wins* saw production designer Syd Cain add another storey to Heatherden Hall, which stood in for the US Embassy under siege in this SAS-themed action thriller.

PRECEDING PAGE: The unlikely combination of *Eraserhead* director David Lynch and *Blazing Saddles*' Mel Brooks brought a stylish black-and-white Victorian world to Shepperton for 1981's *The Elephant Man*.

Years later, Brooks recalled to the *Guardian* how he came to choose Lynch for the job. 'I was taken to the Nuart Theatre, a weird little place on Santa Monica Boulevard, by my producer friend Stuart Cornfeld to see an odd little picture called *Eraserhead*. He was bugging me to see the work of this guy, a new director on the block called David Lynch. It was a beautiful film in black and white, but I still couldn't really believe that this was the director for the project I'd been working on called *The Elephant Man*. But Stuart was convinced, so I met with David. He'd only meet at one place, called Bob's Big Boys, where they serve hamburgers and malt shakes. It was way out in the Valley and I wasn't expecting him to be so polite, but I was rather impressed. He made sense and was very savvy about the changes he wanted.'

Brooks went on to explain his affinity for a project that was, on the face of it, out of character for the comic writer-director. 'It was a problem: how does a guy who is known for the best fart jokes in cinema go on to make *The Elephant Man*? I had all along the line assiduously kept my name from the project. But after this one conversation, David knew I had more to me. I guess it was the outsider aspect that appealed to him. And that's where I think we met, mentally. My films, even if they're comic, they're about: "Let's accept the bizarre. Let's learn more about these creatures, or these Jews." I know the Elephant Man wasn't Jewish, but, to me, the story had all the aspects of anti-Semitism and Merrick had all the traits of the classic wandering Jew.'

Anthony Hopkins was cast as the surgeon, Sir Frederick Treves, and John Hurt, fresh from having his chest burst in spectacular fashion in *Alien*, was cast as Merrick.

The elaborate make-up Hurt was required to wear proved to be extremely problematic, initially delaying production and increasing the budget. This resulted in a schedule change that saw the scenes where Hurt's head is still covered by a cloth sack shot first as the make-up was slowly perfected by artist Christopher Tucker.

Shot in atmospheric black and white by master cinematographer and Hammer veteran Freddie Francis, Lynch's film was initially applauded on release and landed eight Oscar nominations, including Best Film, as well as Best Actor for Hurt and Best Director for Lynch. It won Best Film and Actor at the BAFTAs that year, as well as Best Production Design for Stuart Craig.

The sorry state of film production in the UK at this time was perhaps best exemplified by Blake Edwards taking up residence at Pinewood to make two further Pink Panther movies – after series star Peter Sellers had died. The first of these, *The Trail of the Pink Panther*, utilised outtakes of the actor from earlier films in the series; the second, *The Curse of the Pink Panther*, didn't even bother with that. It did, however, feature Roger Moore in a cameo as a post-cosmetic-surgery version of Clouseau – billed rather splendidly as Turk Thrust. But even he couldn't save the series by then.

Fresh from having his chest burst by an alien in *Alien*, John Hurt donned even more elaborate Oscar-winning make-up for his title role in *The Elephant Man*, here seen conferring on set with his director, David Lynch in 1981.

'That was one of those jobs that came in where I read the script and thought, "Okay, maybe ..."' Moore recalls, 'then they offered £100,000 a day. That went a little way towards tipping the balance. I figured we'd need about four days for all the set-ups so thought my luck was in. In the event, we started at the crack of dawn and finished late into the evening – and that was a wrap. One day's filming – and one day's pay!'

If production was down, the reputation of British cinema was certainly on the rise, with Hugh Hudson's *Chariots of Fire* and Richard Attenborough's long-cherished *Gandhi* dominating both the American Academy Awards and the BAFTAs over the next two years. And if Colin Welland's proclamation, 'The British are coming!'on receiving his Best Screenplay Oscar for the former, proved to be premature and overreaching, it was, at least, well intentioned. In fact, there was little or no immediate effect on film production in the UK, despite all the adulation around the world.

'That was one of those jobs that came in where I read the script and thought, "Okay, maybe ..." then they offered £100,000 a day. That went a little way towards tipping the balance.'

Roger Moore on 'replacing' Peter Sellers in *The Curse of the Pink Panther*

Following in the footsteps of his older brother, Tony Scott (also a commercials director) chose Shepperton to make his feature film debut with *The Hunger*, a stylish, dark, erotic vampire story starring Catherine Deneuve and David Bowie.

In 1982, Shepperton's fortune's looked to be on the up when American producer Sy Weintraub announced, via the UK trade press, his ambitious plans to film between twenty and thirty of Sir Arthur Conan Doyle's Sherlock Holmes short stories, beginning with perhaps the most famous of Holmes' adventures, *The Hound of the Baskervilles*. The wilds of Dartmoor were promptly constructed on the stages of Shepperton, with Douglas Hickox on board as director and Ian Richardson cast as the famous Baker Street detective.

However, due to a rival production being set up at Granada Television and with Conan Doyle's stories now being in the public domain, Weintraub pulled out of his proposed series after only one more film, *The Sign of Four*. Both productions ended up heading straight to television.

Having already played host to Holmes' Dartmoor, the interconnecting A and B stages of Shepperton now found themselves converted into a menacing, magical forest for Neil Jordan's take on Angela Carter's 'The Company of Wolves'. Irish

Producer Sy Weintraub announced ambitious plans to adapt up to thirty of Sir Arthur Conan Doyle's *Sherlock Holmes* series for the big screen. He got as far as two – beginning with 1983's *The Hound Of The Baskervilles*, which saw the stages of Shepperton converted into the forbidding exteriors of Dartmoor.

writer-director Jordan had recently scored a significant art-house hit with his debut movie *Angel*, which introduced the world to actor Stephen Rea. For his sophomore number, Palace Pictures backed his elaborate dark fairy tale.

'We took the two main stages at Shepperton and we knocked down the walls between them, made them into this composite set so there was a forest, and there was a little village, and a little bridge over a river and all these kind of weird environments.'

Neil Jordan creates the dark fairy-tale world of *Company of Wolves*

The titular stars are ready for their close-up on the set of Neil Jordan's *Company of Wolves* (1984). Due to budgetary and safety issues, many of the 'wolves' were played by Belgian Shepherd dogs, who had their fur dyed for their big screen debut.

'*Company of Wolves* was the second movie I made,' Jordan recounts. 'I was working with a designer of brilliance, Anton Furst. When I wrote the script I met various designers and originally I was going to do it with John Beard, who had just come off Terry Gilliam's *Brazil*, but John couldn't do it, so I met Anton Furst and he'd just done one or two location-based films. Basically he was a designer of genius, and he leapt at the chance of making this entirely created world inside a studio. It was almost like making a movie of the thirties or forties, like Max Reinhart's *A Midsummer Night's Dream* or something like that. We had to create this whole world, interior and exterior, on stage and we just went to town on it really.

'We took the two main stages at Shepperton and we knocked down the walls between them, made them into this composite set so there was a forest, and there was a little village, and a little bridge over a river and all these kinds of weird environments. We used the interconnected bit to create an arch of trees into the village. Anton designed these trees with the strangest bark on them. They were like trees designed by Escher or something like that. But they were on rollers so we would shift the trees around the stage to extend the set. So we built the village, we built a series of defined environments that we needed, and we had this forest that we could shift around these standing sets as we needed to.

'It was quite wonderful to work there,' continues Jordan. 'But I have to say the crew didn't have a clue what we were doing. There were these old Shepperton hands. They'd either worked on James Bond, or a lot had come from the latest *Star Wars* or the latest action film, you know. They were utterly confused by what we were up to. That was funny.'

As the decade continued, Ridley Scott would build his own enchanted forest, this time at Pinewood, for *Legend*, the film that was to bring Tom Cruise to Pinewood for the first of what would become many visits. At the same time, he inadvertently

razed the 007 Stage to the ground, due to an electrical malfunction. 'We shot *Legend* at Pinewood Studios,' Scott recounts. 'We built the forest there, which was the centre of the story. The Bond stage was burnt to the ground, but Cubby Broccoli had it up and running within months.

'We built the forest at Pinewood, on the Bond stage which was accidentally burnt to the ground. But with typical British "can do" attitude we only lost three days' filming. Everyone realised we wouldn't let a small thing such as a fire hold us back.'

Ridley Scott recalls a little technical hitch that occurred whilst filming *Legend*

'With typical British "can do" attitude,' Scott continues, recalling the potentially drastic event, 'we only lost three days after this disaster, and were able to get through all the other material I needed by building on the backlot – typical British zeal and enterprise. At that time, before everyone realised we wouldn't let a small thing such as a studio fire hold us back, *Legend* even jokingly became known as *Leg Over*.'

Bond producer Barbara Broccoli remembers the loss of the stage slightly differently. 'It was pretty horrific because we were prepping *A View to a Kill*,' she says, 'and I remember being with Cubby at the White Elephant restaurant on Curzon Street and getting a call. In those days you had no cell phones, I remember a call coming in to the reception for Cubby and going to the reception, picking up the phone and our co-producer Tom Pevsner was on the end of the line and you could hear explosions in the background, which were the Calor Gas cans exploding. It sounded like he was calling from a war zone or something. He said, "The stage is burning down." And I remember being in the restaurant with Cubby a week later and Ridley Scott coming over and saying to Cubby, "I'm very sorry we burnt your stage down."

'Years later, when we were making *Casino Royale*, we finished shooting on the second version of the 007 Stage, and then when we were striking the set we accidentally set the place on fire and it burnt down again.'

'It was terrible,' Michael G. Wilson adds. 'But we had production designer Peter Lamont working on the film and he came up with a plan. It would take so long to rebuild the stage, and then to build and put in the big set we needed inside it, and we didn't have enough time for both. So he said, "As soon as we clear the debris, we'll start building the set *and* build the stage around the set as we go. We'll do both at once." And the executives looked at us like – are you out of your mind? But we did it.'

Ridley Scott moved from Shepperton's H Stage to Pinewood's 007 Stage and built an entire fantasy-world forest for 1984's *Legend*.

Whilst it wasn't a full forest, a full florist, complete with extra-terrestrial plant-based occupant, did converge on the 007 Stage shortly after *Legend* and the subsequent Bond, for the man-eating plant musical *Little Shop of Horrors*, complete with the cream of America's current comedy stars – Bill Murray, Steve Martin, Rick Moranis, John Candy and Christopher Guest.

Having already had the London Docklands stand in for his war-ravaged version of Vietnam, Kubrick decamped to Pinewood to film the volatile interiors of *Full Metal Jacket*.

Kubrick brings the desolation of Vietnam to the backlot of Pinewood for 1987's *Full Metal Jacket.*

Having lost the fourth and final Superman film to Elstree, Pinewood was thrown two lifelines in the form of Stanley Kubrick's Vietnam war epic *Full Metal Jacket*, and James Cameron's outer space war epic *Aliens*.

Said to be increasingly private and reclusive, Kubrick found Pinewood to be perfectly convenient for his latest production, being less than an hour's drive from his home in St Albans. Having already had the London Docklands stand in for his war-ravaged version of Vietnam, the director decamped to Pinewood to film the volatile interiors of the early training sections of the movie, highlighting the verbal brutality of R. Lee Ermey's drill sergeant. Ermey was the real deal in that he had been an actual drill sergeant, and Kubrick allowed him free rein to let fly with a constant stream of obscenities designed to dehumanise his new raw recruits. Not that the director didn't still demand take after take from his actor, with new derogatory epithets expected every time.

James Cameron, meanwhile, coming off the success of his career-launching *The Terminator*, was being charged with a huge budget and the opportunity to follow up Ridley Scott's *Alien*, taking Scott's haunted house movie in space and redefining it as an all-out war movie in space, one that was in its own way as much about Vietnam as Kubrick's was.

Veteran art director Terry Ackland-Snow recalls working with the very demanding Cameron.

'I know of one situation that was very challenging for the production designer, Peter Lamont,' Ackland-Snow continues. 'We needed to cut £250,000 out of the budget. We only had three sets left to build and one of those sets was gonna cost £250,000 so we wanted to cut that one out. And our producer Gale Anne Hurd, who was also Cameron's wife at the time, said, "That's great." Jim Cameron wasn't there because it was just a budget meeting, but then he arrived and said, "Carry on, carry on, I'm only the director. Don't worry about it." And his wife said, "Oh, we've saved £250,000

James Cameron inspects his
own alien world for *Aliens* (1986),
recreated on stage at Pinewood,
six years after Ridley Scott used
Shepperton to similar effect.

out of the construction budget." Jim says, "That's good, how?" She says, "Terry suggested cutting this set out." So they did. And they did save £250,000.'

Shepperton underwent a major refurbishment and upgrading across the whole site, which was ready just in time for *2010* – the movie, not the year.

Despite having lost one of its sets, *Aliens* proved to be both hugely influential and hugely successful, bringing a very profitable and large-scale production to Pinewood.

Around this time, Shepperton found itself under new ownership. Like the Kordas and the Boultings before (and the Scotts to follow), John and Barry Lee were brothers, former studio electricians who had built up Lee Studios in the London suburb of Wembley.

When the Lees bought Shepperton, they also bought out The Who and thus bought back the old house, as well as reacquiring H Stage, which had been leased to the local council as a proposed – but never realised – housing site. Determined to make the studio a fully going concern once more, the brothers renamed it Lee International Studios, Shepperton. They also undertook a major refurbishment and upgraded the whole site, which was ready just in time for *2010* – the movie, not the year.

Stanley Kubrick had passed on the chance to film a follow-up to his now highly regarded original *2001: A Space Odyssey*, and the (thankless) task had fallen to *Outland*'s Peter Hyams. Before he took the job, Hyams insisted on seeking Kubrick's blessing. A lengthy phone call between the two followed, with Kubrick spending all his time quizzing Hyams over various shots from *Outland* – his de facto blessing, in essence.

Shortly after Hyams wrapped up his science fiction opus, which saw the mysterious monolith once again grace the stages of Shepperton, studio veteran David Lean briefly returned to complete *A Passage to India*. The film would turn out to be the director's final work. He did begin pre-production on *Nostromo*, his long-cherished adaptation of Joseph Conrad's novel, whilst still based at Shepperton, although by now he was so frail that insurers required a more than willing Martin Scorsese to be named as a potential stand-in. As it transpired, Lean died before the production could be realised.

Amidst all this, Pinewood celebrated its fiftieth anniversary in 1986 with a TV special, despite the insecurity over its future.

Camera on shoulder, James
Cameron gets down amongst the
grunts, on the set of *Aliens* (1986).

Director Peter Hyams steps into
Stanley Kubrick's considerable
shoes for the sequel *2010*, seen here
with co-stars Roy Scheider and John
Lithgow.

RIGHT: Eric Idle and Robbie
Coltrane. They're *Nuns on the Run*
in an empty studio lot.

Since its inception in 1957, the Eady Levy had ensured that a certain percentage
of the finances generated at UK box offices would be directed back into film
production. In 1985, under Margaret Thatcher's Conservative government, this tax
was abolished. Concurrently, the government was responsible for cancelling a 25 per
cent tax break for film investors in the country, placing the future of British film
production in further jeopardy. Ironically, 1985 was also named British Film Year.

By October 1987, Pinewood was the last fully serviced studio in the country.
Reluctantly, studio head Cyril Howard reached the conclusion that, in an era of
dwindling production, this was no longer tenable. He assembled the studio staff
on one of the sound stages and made the announcement that Pinewood was going
'four-wall' – from now on, productions would have to provide their own crews. This
effectively reduced those on the Pinewood payroll from around 500 down to just 145.

Kenneth Branagh had made a name for himself as the young bright hope of British theatre. He chose to house his debut film production at Shepperton. He would return there many times in the years to come.

'It became a different place when it went four-wall,' Bond producer Michael G. Wilson remembers. 'That was the big change. All the people that had been working there for life, they were all let go. It was a really rough time for the people that worked there, but most of them became independent contractors. You didn't have an integrated film studio any more. You didn't have everything at your fingertips. You had to bring everything in.'

Belfast-born Kenneth Branagh had made a name for himself as the young bright hope of British theatre. When he decided to transfer the recent success of his Renaissance Theatre Group to the big screen, he chose to house their debut production at Shepperton. He would return there many times in the years to come.

Branagh's first movie as director was an adaptation of Shakespeare's *Henry V*, previously filmed to Oscar-nominated acclaim by his idol Laurence Olivier in 1944 (a man Branagh himself would play many years later in *My Week with Marilyn*, shot at Pinewood). Branagh set his entire movie within two of the sound stages at Shepperton, using the backlot fields to recreate the Battle of Agincourt.

Having already conquered the stage and found fame on television, Branagh's debut movie proved a huge success, and saw him duplicate Olivier's achievement when he was nominated for Best Actor at the following year's Oscars. (Unlike Olivier, Branagh also received a nod for Best Director.)

But by the time Eric Idle, Robbie Coltrane and director Jonathan Lynn showed up at Shepperton to make the Handmade Films comedy *Nuns on the Run* shortly after Branagh and Co. exited the lot, they found themselves the only film in production there. Lynn later referred to it as 'a ghost studio', pointing out that the restaurant had to be specially opened to accommodate them.

As for Pinewood, the studio was once again in need of a hero. This time it didn't come in the shape of a Superman. This time, it would be a Dark Knight.

Henry V, King Charles VI; Kenneth Branagh starts with the lens – here, gearing up to make the move to film director, with Paul Scofield in 1989's *Henry V.*

TIME FOR A NEW HERO

I F *SUPERMAN* HAD SPENT OVER FIVE YEARS

in development a decade before, *Batman* would take around twice that

amount of time, the rights having been snapped up from DC Comics shortly after

the Man of Steel's record-breaking big-screen debut. Batman, an altogether darker

kind of superhero, was just a year younger than his comic-book stablemate, having

first appeared in an issue of *Detective Comics* in 1939.

Like Superman, his on-screen life was initially limited to a 1940s movie serial and numerous cartoons. Unlike the Son of Krypton, he had also featured in a hugely successful TV series, designed to capture the mood of the swinging sixties. An expanded version of that show, starring Adam West as the Caped Crusader, was released as a feature film in 1966, but Batman had never really been given a proper big-screen treatment.

Producers Peter Guber and Jon Peters now aimed to change that.

Thirty-year-old former Disney animator Tim Burton had scored a big hit with his debut feature, *Pee-wee's Big Adventure*, and built on that success by providing Warner Bros with another major hit via his follow-up, *Beetlejuice*, a wildly imaginative post-life comedy that had made tremendous use of its lead, comic actor Michael Keaton.

Still, the two of them weren't the obvious choice to revitalise the comic-book movie. Since the days of Reeve's *Superman* a decade before, the genre had more or less imploded, not helped by the weaker and cheaper approach that the Salkinds had taken to the *Superman* sequels.

At the same time, in the comic-book world itself, there had recently been something of a revolution, with the advent of the more adult-orientated graphic novel adding not only a decidedly darker tone, but a new legitimacy to the form, something that had been spearheaded by Frank Miller's reinvention of the character of Batman in *The Dark Knight Returns*. This was to prove a major influence on Burton's take on Bruce Wayne and his crime-fighting alter ego.

'I don't think it was a coincidence that the project was greenlighted after the first weekend of *Beetlejuice*,' Burton said at the time. 'Warner Bros have always been supportive of me. From their point of view, Batman was a visual project and they think of me in that context. Because my background was in animation and this was a film based on a comic strip, they seemed to think that was a good connection. Also,

the project had been around so long it had become somewhat of a dinosaur – almost as if it had a curse on it. Everyone said, "Great project," but at the same time they were thinking, "If it's such a great project, why are you having so much trouble getting it made?" So I think I was given the job for all of these reasons – I had an idea as to how it should be done.'

Burton went on to explain his take on the material. 'I felt it should not be too dark or too campy – I was right in the middle about it. I pitched "true" Batman – not the TV series and yet not this extremely dark, unhumorous thing.'

Initially, the young director bringing his *Beetlejuice* star, Michael Keaton, on board as the Bat proved divisive with fans and critics alike, resulting in some 50,000 angry protest letters arriving at Warner Bros.

'I thought that Michael was a very interesting choice,' Burton explained. 'I had considered a lot of people for the role, but I could not see them putting on a Batsuit.

Director Tim Burton explores the dark with his Dark Knight, 1989. 'I felt it should not be too dark or too campy ... I pitched "true" Batman – not the TV series yet not this extremely dark, unhumorous thing.'

PRECEDING PAGE: Tim Burton signals a different kind of Bat.

The idea of someone like Michael dressing up as a bat made a lot more sense to me than someone with the classic comic-book image.'

In a move to assuage fans, and one that echoed the Salkinds' approach from years before, the production secured a major box office name for the bad guy. Jack Nicholson was perfectly cast as the Joker, a role that legend has it had the likes of Willem Dafoe, James Woods, John Lithgow and even David Bowie in the frame. Robin Williams was said to be on hold whilst Nicholson deliberated. But accept he did, and – again in a move that echoed the Salkinds' enormous payday for Nicholson's friend and Hollywood neighbour Marlon Brando – he was paid so much that he would reportedly walk on set each morning saying, 'Another day – another $250,000,' generally accompanied by a world-weary sigh. (Nicholson also had percentage points in not only this film but the sequels he didn't appear in, and subsequently parlayed his original $10 million fee into anywhere between $60 million and $100 million – still to this day the highest any actor has ever earned from a single movie.)

'The thought of shooting *Batman* in some New York location just didn't feel right to me. Pinewood had a perfect set-up for building the sets we needed.'

Burton brings his Bat to Buckinghamshire

The film took up residence at Pinewood. 'I wanted to shoot in England for several reasons,' Burton explained. 'It started out as a financial consideration, although soon after we made the decision the dollar fell and that became a moot point. But, economics aside, England had a lot to offer. Pinewood had the space available – which is difficult to find in LA, because everything gets booked up. We probably would have wound up having to shoot on location somewhere and I did not like that idea at all. The characters in the movie are so extreme that I felt it was important to set them in an arena that was specifically designed for them. I like *Superman* on an emotional level, but because it was shot on location in New York, I don't think it captured the visual quality of the comic book.

'The thought of shooting *Batman* in some New York location just didn't feel right to me. Pinewood had a perfect set-up for building the sets we needed – a big outdoor area with a street already laid in. So all of the groundwork had already been laid and we designed Gotham City with that space in mind. I also wanted to shoot there because with a big-budget movie there is so much hype and pressure, I felt I would be able to focus better if I was away from all of that – and I was right.'

Michael Keaton consults with his director Burton between shots in *Batman* (1989). 'The idea of someone like Michael dressing up as a bat made a lot more sense to me than someone with the classic comic-book image.'

Production designer Anton Furst, who had previously built a magical forest at Shepperton for Neil Jordan's *Company of Wolves*, was the man charged with taking over the backlot at Pinewood to recreate the gloomy towers and run-down streets of Gotham City, creating one of the largest sets ever in Pinewood's history, indeed the largest exterior set built in Europe since *Cleopatra* back in the early 1960s.

An admirer of his work on *Company of Wolves*, Burton brought Furst on board in February of 1988, leaving him and his team just three months to construct Gotham City, which was to be a mixture of miniatures and a huge five-and-a-half-block street set. 'The skyscrapers of the city are supposed to be up to one thousand feet high,' the designer explained to *Cinefex* magazine at the time. 'But, from the beginning, I knew that we were only going to be building at most the first fifty feet of the buildings in full scale. The "top" of the entire city was slated to be done with models. By far the biggest challenge was figuring out what should be built full scale and how we would best achieve enormously complicated effects within the infrastructure of full-scale sets as well as model sets in several different scales. It was very difficult.'

'The Gotham street was nearly a quarter of a mile long. Absolutely enormous. It had everything required in it.'

Terry Ackland-Snow on bringing Gotham City to life on the Pinewood backlot

The Gotham City street set – at that time the largest exterior set ever built at Pinewood.

Going back to the original comic books, Furst's Gotham had a 1940s noir feel to it, with buildings towering oppressively over and into the streets. 'As Tim characterised it, it was just a hell that had erupted through the pavement and kept on going.'

'For me it was very exciting,' recalls Terry Ackland-Snow, whom Furst brought on board as art director. 'I'd worked on the budget of the film with producer Chris Kenny and we spent about four months on the budget and much to my surprise in Los Angeles they accepted it. Then I met with Anton Furst on Good Friday, and then immediately after the Easter holidays we went walking along the backlot to see where we were going to build Gotham City. Anton saw the back of a washing machine and said to me: "Oh, that'll make a good museum entrance." I didn't understand, but what he meant was that the detail of the motor was what he wanted to put as the entrance so that's how we designed it. Anton was a think-of-it designer, if you see what I mean. And Les Tomkins and I were the workers.

'The Gotham street was nearly a quarter of a mile long,' Ackland-Snow continues. 'It was absolutely enormous. It had everything required in it. American cars had to be in it. But Tim Burton wanted it to look quite dark, like the comic-strip stuff.'

Ackland-Snow had previous experience of creating a full-scale American street on

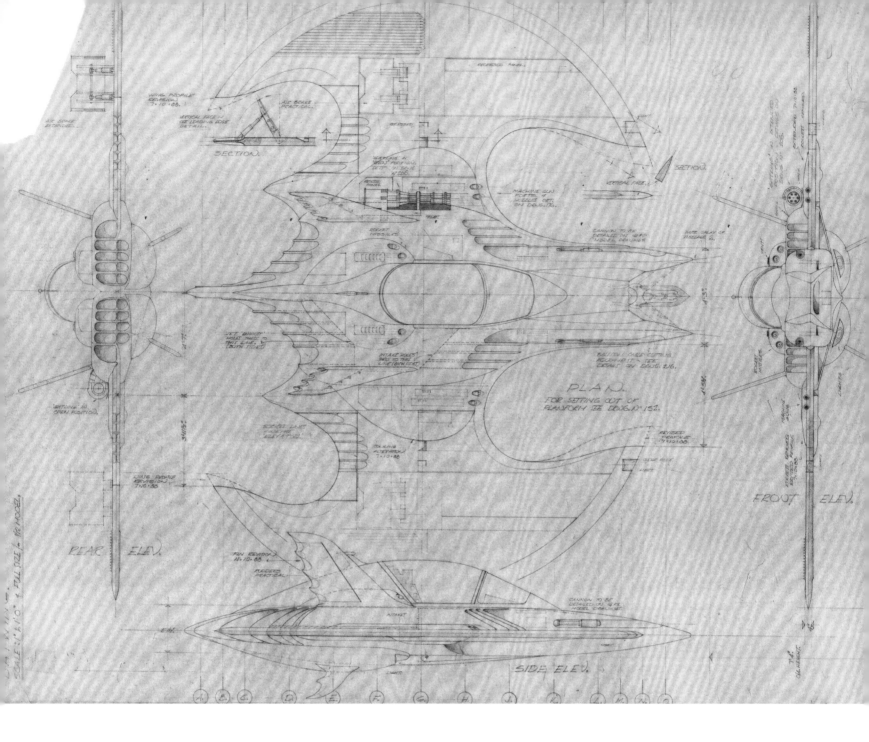

the Pinewood backlot, having done the same thing years earlier for *Supergirl*.

'It wasn't quite as big as the Gotham City set,' he says, 'but it was very long and to make it look as if it went on longer we built the end part of the street in perspective and that was raised up to about eight feet high. And I can remember in those days people used to take their families to look at the set and drive on all the roads, and one guy drove along it and then he sped off the end of it. He thought it was getting smaller and then the next minute he's dropped eight feet.'

Ultimately, Furst's city streets took up most of Pinewood's nineteen-acre backlot and took five months to build with a crew of around 250 workmen. 'It was pretty hairy anyway, building sets fifty feet high, half a mile long, and then plastering and painting all of that,' Furst explained. 'Also, the way I had designed it – with the

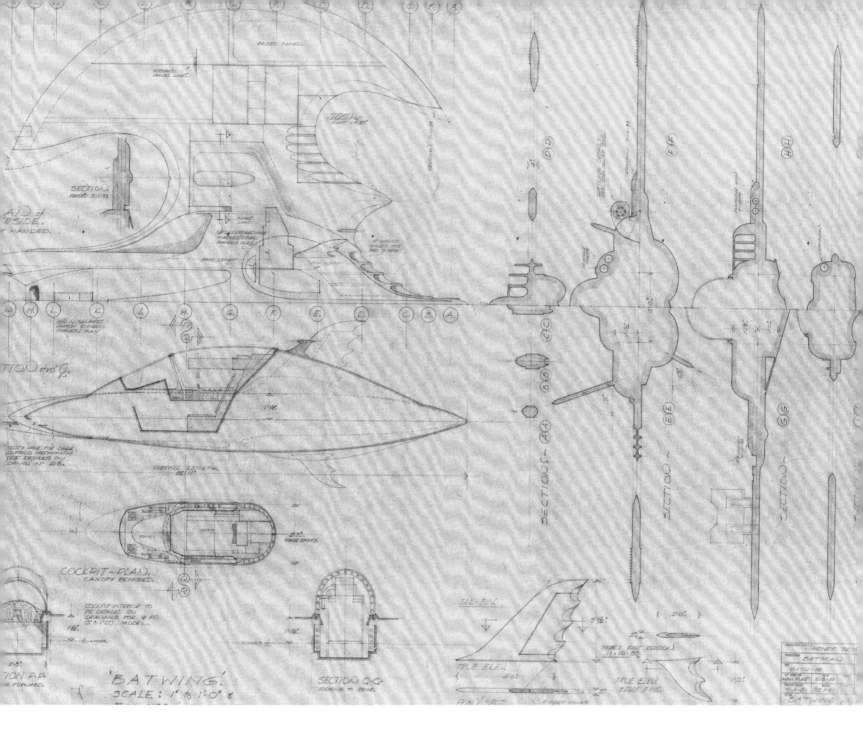

buildings cantilevering forward – made the construction a bit more difficult because the preparation below the ground level had to be almost as substantial as what we built above ground. All of the footings and bearings had to be set into concrete. And because it was so high we had to build the set to withstand up to force eight wind conditions – and that is tons of weight.'

As well as commandeering the backlot, *Batman* also took over most of the studio's sound stages, with the 007 Stage reserved for the Batcave. 'I came up with a *Phantom of the Opera* concept,' said Furst, 'whereby the Batcave is actually in the foundations of the city with the piles of the skyscrapers and sewer pipes and things like that coming down through the rock structures. That made it more interesting and also more dangerous – which fitted in with Batman because everything he does is on the edge of disaster.'

This Batman didn't just have a 'mobile', he had a 'wing' as well. Early designs of the Batwing, seen in the climax of Burton's first *Batman* (1989).

Whilst Furst was busy building a city, Burton turned to Oscar-nominated costume designer Bob Ringwood to build a better Batsuit. Ringwood, who had never read a single Batman comic, began his research by buying a whole stack of them and making his way through. 'In talking to Tim Burton, I knew he wanted to make this Batman more the Dark Knight of the later comics and lose the camp TV elements, and also lose the gauche style of the early cartoons. So I looked at more of the recent comics than the others and based the look of the costume on these, hoping we could recreate the Dark Knight look in three dimensions. Then I closed the comics and started thinking about why a man would dress up as a bat – the whole idea is absurd – and I decided that to make it work, I had to come up with a bat that was dark and mysterious and sexy. At that point I forgot the comic and went my own way.'

'I said, "I'd like to be in charge of the biggest prop in the film industry." And we didn't even mention the Batmobile, he just said, "You've got it."'

Terry Ackland-Snow gets to build the Batmobile

Creating the costume was a case of trial and error for Ringwood and his team, not just in capturing the right look but in designing a suit that was functional for Keaton to both wear and perform in. But with the actor suited and booted, as with Superman before him, the cape proved to be an issue. A first attempt made of rubber, to match the general look of the suit, simply didn't move well, and after experimenting with various other fabrics, Batman's main cape was eventually made of Venetian wool, spray-painted with wet rubber. Around forty capes were eventually constructed, of varying length and functionality. To complete the look, Ringwood based Batman's boots on some 'butch-looking' Nike trainers, and recruited Nike to make them to his specific design.

The cowl completed the look, with ears that Ringwood described as 'like the "go faster" fins on 1950s American cars'. At one point Burton tried the mask on himself. 'I put the head on and it really was a bizarre feeling. I could not hear and my peripheral vision was affected. Michael is a bit claustrophobic, too, which made it worse for him. The costume put him in a dark, Batman-like mood, though, so he was able to use that to his advantage.'

Whilst Batman was getting his suit and Jack Nicholson was helping design his Joker make-up, Anton Furst and his team were busy building Gotham in miniature, as well as a certain key player in the Bat mythology – the Batmobile.

'I said to Anton, "I'd like to be in charge of the biggest prop in the film industry,"' Terry Ackland-Snow remembers. 'And we didn't even mention the Batmobile, he just said, "You've got it."

'We literally bought some old American convertible cars, and we did a clay model of it. Then we developed it from there and it was very, very exciting to build because everybody wanted to see it. Tim Burton was quite hands-on because he described what he wanted to see and we did it. But I can remember showing him this big polystyrene sculpture, which was about twenty-nine feet long, and he looked at it and said, "It's really good, but how do they get in?" And I'd forgotten to design doors on it.'

'To me the Batmobile was a pure piece of expressionism,' Furst said, elaborating on his design for the car. 'I tried to give it that "knight in armour" look, taking elements of the speed machines from the Utah salt flats of the '40s, the Corvette Stingrays of the '50s, and combining those elements with jet aircraft components to create one cohesive machine. In a way the Batmobile was a more hairy project than building those huge sets. It certainly worried me the most.'

As well as struggling with the Batmobile, Furst was also supervising the building of numerous miniatures on various other stages at Pinewood, including a scale reconstruction of his exterior Gotham street set. Legendary visual effects supervisor (and *Superman* veteran) Derek Meddings was brought in to oversee the model unit, relocating his Meddings Magic Camera Company from its usual home at Shepperton at the director's request. 'Tim really wanted the miniatures to be shot in the same studio as the live action,' Meddings explained to *Cinefex* at the time, 'and for us it was advantageous to have the director close at hand – we could walk over a couple of stages to get an okay instead of making a half-hour drive. Also, I know Pinewood very well – I did five Bond films there and they have a really good set-up for shooting miniatures.'

Derek Meddings' 'miniature' Gotham street set was forty feet long and comprised fourteen buildings that ranged from twenty to thirty feet tall.

Meddings' miniature street set was forty feet long and comprised fourteen buildings that ranged from twenty to thirty feet tall. One of these buildings was Gotham Cathedral, where the film's climax was to take place. Even at thirty feet, this miniature was not enough to accommodate the action required, so a further sixty-foot model was built by Meddings and his team, partly on its side to house it on the sound stage.

Sometimes, however, solutions to problems proved to be remarkably simple. For the sequence where Batman chases the Joker into the bell tower up a seemingly endless staircase, a forty-foot model of the staircase was built, but was still deemed not to be 'endless' enough. So a photograph was taken looking down at the model, reduced and laid on the floor, to create a feeling of the stairs going on forever.

The design of the bell tower was clearly a nod to Hitchcock's *Vertigo* on Burton's part, but it was not the only Hitchcock reference Anton Furst managed to incorporate into his designs for Gotham.

'I've always liked the house in Hitchcock's *Psycho*,' the designer admitted, 'so I topped off the cathedral with the top of the Hitchcock house and we ended up with this really eccentric building with deep-pitched gothic roofs and spires coming off the top. It really had to be a forbidding-looking thing in my view – as if it had been closed down and locked up because God left the city years ago.'

Upon its much-anticipated release in the summer of 1989, *Batman*, one of the largest productions in Pinewood's history, went on to become the highest-grossing film of the year worldwide.

Tim Burton stands proudly atop his Batmobile in 1989, having rebuilt both Gotham and the superhero movie genre.

MANY HAPPY RETURNS

B Y THE START OF THE PRE-MILLENNIAL DECADE, Pinewood was still attracting large-scale productions, if intermittently, and Gotham City was still dominating the studio's backlot, having been left standing for the hopeful return of the Caped Crusader. Sadly, though, it was struck when Tim Burton decided to film his sequel, *Batman Returns*, at Warner Bros' Burbank Studios in the US.

Pop video director David Fincher came to the studio to make his feature debut, continuing the *Alien* franchise's relationship with the studio on *Alien 3*. The 007 Stage was converted into a massive monastery in a distant part of the galaxy, complete with rampaging xenomorph, Sigourney Weaver and a largely British supporting cast that included Charles Dance, Pete Postlethwaite and Brian Glover. Despite a troubled production, the film once again received an Oscar nomination in the Best Visual Effects category.

Harrison Ford took on the role of Tom Clancy's CIA analyst Jack Ryan in *Patriot Games*, a film that changed at least one aspect of Pinewood for ever. When the large boardroom in the main hall was converted into two rooms, the studio decided to leave it that way, and there is a large and a smaller boardroom to this day. (Jack Ryan the character would return to Pinewood in 2013 for *Jack Ryan* the movie, directed by Kenneth Branagh. But by this time, Ford had been replaced in the role, first by Ben Affleck then, in this case, by Chris Pine.)

In the early '90s over at Shepperton, large-scale film productions such as Franco Zeffirelli's *Hamlet*, starring Mel Gibson, jostled for stage space with a mixture of pop promos and such TV shows as *Alas Smith & Jones* and *Red Dwarf*.

By sheer serendipity, 1990 saw two variations on the Robin Hood legend shooting in the UK at both studios. Pinewood landed the lower-budget Patrick Bergin-starring *Robin Hood*, whilst Shepperton found itself playing host to the bigger, of budget and profile both, *Robin Hood: Prince of Thieves*. Fresh from his multi-Oscar-winning western *Dances with Wolves*, Kevin Costner donned tights and picked up bow, alongside Morgan Freeman and Mary Elizabeth Mastrantonio, against the delightful scenery-chewing of Alan Rickman as the Sheriff of Nottingham.

The film went over schedule by several months but proved to be a huge success upon release, with Bryan Adams's love theme from the film, 'Everything I Do (I Do It For You)', holding the number one position on the UK pop charts for a record-breaking sixteen weeks, accompanied by a synergistic video that included numerous clips

Kenneth Branagh directs John Gielgud in his ambitious production of *Hamlet* (1996).

PRECEDING PAGE: Tom Cruise enjoys hanging out once again at Pinewood for *Mission: Impossible* (1996).

from the movie and featured Adams and band playing the song 'on location' in Sherwood Forest. Needless to say, in an era when the pop promo had become a dominant sales tool for movies, the success of the single boosted the success of the film considerably in the UK and beyond.

Robin Hood: Prince of Thieves was significant for one other reason – it brought Sean Connery to Shepperton for a brief appearance at the end of the movie as King Richard, back from the Crusades. For his thirty-second turn, Connery walked away with $500,000. It was his second appearance in a Robin Hood movie, having previously played an ageing Robin in Richard Lester's splendid *Robin and Marian* back in 1976.

'I was totally shattered by this man who seemed to me not only to have genius but to have a unique genius ... he was able to grasp my attention, either emotionally or cerebrally, however he chose.'
Richard Attenborough on his lifelong fascination with Charlie Chaplin

The versatility of Pinewood was demonstrated once again when the ornamental gardens were used as the title 'character' in an adaptation of Frances Hodgson Burnett's classic children's story *The Secret Garden*, at the same time, the Carry On team returned to their natural home for one last hurrah. *Carry On Columbus* was an ill-judged attempt to jump on the back of two other movies being released that same year to tie in with the five hundredth anniversary of Christopher Columbus's discovery of America – Ridley Scott's *1492: Conquest of Paradise*, and *Christopher Columbus: The Discovery*, with Marlon Brando and Tom Selleck. Peter Rogers and Gerald Thomas were back in their roles of producer and director respectively, but sadly, very few of the original team were even alive to revive theirs, while some of those who were were reluctant to come on board.

The film banged the final nail into the lid of the Carry On coffin, showing just how much audiences' tastes had changed over the last couple of decades. (To be fair, all three Columbus movies flopped that year, proving that the Carry On team weren't the only ones to overestimate the public's appetite for celebrating Columbus's significant anniversary.)

Around this time, Pinewood decided to lighten its dependence on large-scale movie productions by expanding its horizons with its first live TV broadcasts. The BBC's Saturday morning children's show *Parallel 9* was an experiment for the studio, but one that proved so successful the series booked in for what turned out to be a three-year run.

Director Kevin Reynolds confers with Kevin Costner and Morgan Freeman between takes on *Robin Hood: Prince of Thieves* (1991).

The 500-year anniversary of Christopher Columbus's discovery of America led to the resurrection of the Carry On franchise, with 1992's *Carry On Columbus*. Original series director Gerald Thomas returned, alongside newcomers such as American comic Larry Miller.

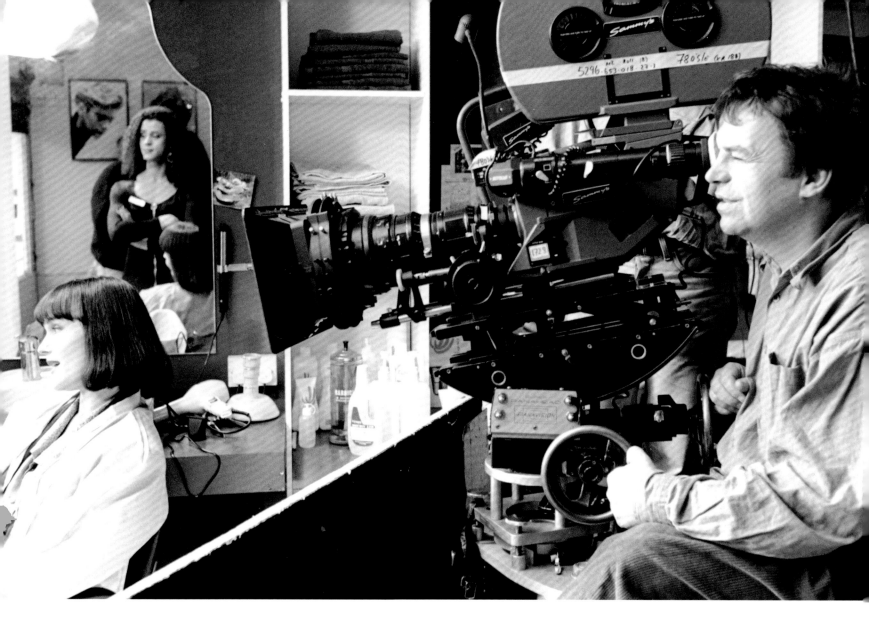

Neil Jordan partly shot *The Crying Game* (1992) at Shepperton. Jordan went on to win an Oscar for his screenplay, and an acting nomination for lead Jaye Davidson (seen here in the mirror).

RIGHT: Richard Attenborough was back once again at Shepperton to realise his long-cherished dream project, *Chaplin* (1992). Lead actor Robert Downey Jr played Charlie and landed an Oscar nomination for his work.

Richard Attenborough, meanwhile, found himself back at his favourite studio, Shepperton, to bring his long-cherished film of the life of Charlie Chaplin to the big screen. For the lead role he cast young American actor Robert Downey Jr (who would return to the studio many years later as both Sherlock Homes and as a key member of Marvel's Avengers).

Attenborough later explained his lifelong fascination with the comedian to author Gareth Owen. 'When I was ten or eleven my father brought me up to London as he had meetings,' the director recalled, 'and he said, "I know somebody who you'll like very much. Let's walk along to the London Pavilion." Which is what we did and saw *The Gold Rush*. And I was totally shattered by this man who seemed to me not only to have genius but to have a unique genius … he was able to grasp my attention, either emotionally or cerebrally, however he chose. He was able to make you laugh or cry. I thought he was just incredible. And so right from that age I was fascinated by him.'

Shepperton was certainly still attracting successful films, including Neil Jordan's breakout movie *The Crying Game*, which earned the writer/director a Best Original Screenplay Oscar.

Hugh Grant and the woman who doesn't notice it's raining, Andie MacDowell, in the much loved and hugely successful *Four Weddings and a Funeral* (1994).

Shot in part at Shepperton Studios, *Four Weddings and a Funeral* went on to become the highest-grossing British film in the US ever (at that time), and launched the international careers of both star Hugh Grant and writer Richard Curtis.

The Muppets, meanwhile, recruited Michael Caine to Shepperton for their *Christmas Carol* and delivered a modern seasonal classic.

Pinewood, however, was dealt a significant blow in 1992. Julia Roberts, at that time one of the biggest stars in the world, was scheduled to star in the romantic comedy *Shakespeare in Love*. Stages had been booked, elaborate Elizabethan sets constructed and crews hired. But Roberts would only make the movie if Daniel Day Lewis would star opposite her in the role of the young Will Shakespeare. At the eleventh hour, Day Lewis withdrew from the project and Roberts, true to her word, followed, and the production was shuttered. (It was resurrected some six years later over at Shepperton with Gwyneth Paltrow and Joseph Fiennes in for Roberts and Day Lewis, and went on to win the Best Picture Oscar in 1999.)

Shortly following the collapse of this first pass at *Shakespeare in Love*, in late 1992,

Steve Jaggs took over from Cyril Howard as Pinewood's managing director. Whilst he found the studio somewhat down, he believed that it was by no means out, and set about renovating it to its former glories. One of the first major bookings under Jaggs's new regime saw Tom Cruise return for Neil Jordan's *Interview with the Vampire*. 'I did one movie at Pinewood, *Interview with the Vampire*,' Jordan recounts. 'And it was very interesting because it was almost like making an independent movie on a huge budget. We built a big Paris street set, a brilliant street, built a lot of the interiors we needed. A huge graveyard set, and the Theatre of the Vampires, which we built on the Bond stage, designed by Dante Ferretti, which was great.

'It was a much bigger film for me than what I'd done before. And it was kind of unique circumstances because it was a very popular book and it had two big stars and I was given the freedom that I wanted by Warner Bros to make it as I saw fit. It was a rather big enterprise at the time. Nothing like the films they make now, but at the time it cost us $70 million or $80 million. We shot in New Orleans, then we moved to Paris and we ended up at Pinewood.'

Co-starring Brad Pitt, this take on Anne Rice's hugely popular Vampire Chronicles

Judi Dench may have had to spend hours in make-up and hair for her role as Queen Elizabeth I in 1998's *Shakespeare in Love* – but, at the end of the day, she did go home with an Oscar.

novels showed not only just how much Cruise's personal star had risen since his last time in the UK shooting *Legend*, nearly a decade earlier, but also how the nature of celebrity and its relationship with the media was changing. Cruise not only came with a very public display of personal security around the studio, but covered walkways were constructed between dressing rooms, trailers and the stages to avoid the actor being snapped by the now ever-present paparazzi.

'There was a lot of press interest about the movie because the book was so popular and because I'd cast two very, very big stars really,' Jordan remembers. 'We kind of hid ourselves from the world as we were making it. We shot in San Francisco, and in New Orleans, and in America there was huge press interest in us. I think Anne Rice, who's a popular novelist, was at her peak and there was a huge following before the movie for the book, you know. There was interest in what I would do with the film, who would play Lestat and was Tom Cruise correct for playing Lestat and all that sort of stuff. So we did suffer a huge paparazzi onslaught there, but we were helped by the fact that we were shooting at night so sometimes we could use black curtains to block off streets.'

'There was a lot of press interest about the movie because the book was so popular and because I'd cast two very, very big stars. We kind of hid ourselves from the world as we were making it.'
Director Neil Jordan on hiding out at Pinewood whilst bringing *Interview with the Vampire* to life

With all the attention on the film, Jordan soon found himself holed up at Pinewood and facing a very public backlash from author Anne Rice herself, who initially criticised his choice of Cruise as Lestat (a position she reversed in an equally public manner upon seeing the film).

'It was more that the character was so ingrained in people's imaginations who had read the book,' Jordan says in retrospect, 'so everybody had an opinion as to who should play the role. And Tom is such a great actor that the minute he's given a challenge he will rise to it, if you know what I mean. I think the more opposition to his casting was vocalised, the more intense his engagement with the part became. He's such a big star because he is a very good actor, and in the end I thought he gave a great performance.'

Meanwhile, Angelina Jolie also made her first appearance at the studio that same year, in Ian Softley's teen computer-hacking adventure *Hackers*, which saw the young cast careening around the studio on roller blades. (Jolie would return to

Kenneth Branagh may have brought the Bard's works to Shepperton, but Joseph Fiennes brought the man himself – albeit in an early draft – in 1998's multi-Oscar-winning *Shakespeare in Love*, a film that years before had been scheduled to film at Pinewood with Daniel Day Lewis cast as the young Will.

the studios later, both as the tomb-raiding Lara Croft, and the Sleeping Beauty-worrying Maleficent.)

And, having walked away from *Shakespeare in Love*, even Julia Roberts returned to Pinewood in 1993, in the title role of *Mary Reilly*, with director Stephen Frears's film retelling the Jekyll and Hyde story from the point of view of the doctor's maid.

'We went for Julia Roberts, and made the only movie where she doesn't smile,' recalls producer Iain Smith, laughing. 'Actually she does, there's one scene where she gives a very slight smile. But we were playing against type in the sense that her unique selling point was smiling through the tears. That was her big thing. I don't think Mary Reilly cries once, or smiles.

Guests to John Cleese's Pinewood-based zoo included Tom Cruise and family, as well as Princess Diana and young princes William and Harry.

John Cleese brought *Fierce Creatures* (1997), his unofficial sequel to *A Fish Called Wanda*, to Pinewood, where he built a fully functioning zoo, populated with many exotic animals – including himself as a kangaroo.

'But it was a very ambitious undertaking,' Smith continues. 'We built two Edinburgh streets. This was at a time just before the emergence of the digital world, so we filled the 007 Stage with a cobbled Edinburgh street and building facades. It was really quite something. Nowadays we wouldn't do that. We'd build foreground and mid-ground and put the rest in digitally. But Stuart Craig was our wonderful designer. He used false perspective and foreground miniatures. He used a lot of very traditional methodologies to achieve the effect.'

Indeed, it was a time for many returns to Pinewood.

Gerry Anderson was back for the first time since *Space: 1999* with his latest TV series, the ambitious cops-in-space tale *Space Precinct*. Based at Pinewood for live-action shooting and Shepperton for its special-effects work, *Space Precinct* was a major production and filmed for a full season of twenty-five episodes.

Unfortunately, the series did not find the same favour – or fervour – of Anderson's work of old and was cancelled after that first year.

Also returning to the studio was Sean Connery, who took on the role of a somewhat older King Arthur, facing up to a decidedly younger and more dashing Lancelot, in the form of Richard Gere. Jerry Zucker's reinvention of the Arthurian legend, *First Knight*, saw Camelot come to the backlot courtesy of John Box's elaborate production design.

The Loch Ness Monster – previously seen in the Paddock Tank in 1969 for Billy Wilder's *The Private Life of Sherlock Holmes* – was also back, this time playing

opposite Ted Danson and Joely Richardson in the children's adventure *Loch Ness*.

John Cleese, however, was coming to Pinewood for the first time; years before, he had moved his production of *A Fish Called Wanda* away from the studio to Twickenham shortly before the production was due to begin. Now he booked into Pinewood for a sort of follow-up. Originally titled *Death Fish 2* but soon to be known as *Fierce Creatures*, the film reunited the principal cast from *Wanda* – Cleese, Jamie Lee Curtis, Kevin Kline and Michael Palin – but as different characters in a different story. It also saw Cleese constructing a full-scale, fully functioning private zoo on the studio's backlot, complete with an array of exotic animals. The zoo proved to be very popular with celebrity visitors, including Princess Diana, who brought along Princes William and Harry, the Duchess of York with Princesses Beatrice and Eugenie, and Tom Cruise and family.

Cruise was back at Pinewood for his first film as producer, a big-screen adaptation of the 1960s TV spy show *Mission: Impossible*, which saw the actor blown across the 007

Sylvester Stallone discusses keeping the helmet on with director Danny Cannon on the first big-screen adaptation of the classic British comic book anti-hero, *Judge Dredd* (1995), shot largely at Shepperton.

LEFT: The Zoo That John Built, *Fierce Creatures* (1997).

FOLLOWING PAGE: Tom Cruise, clearly enjoying himself, hanging off the back of a speeding train on Pinewood's 007 Stage for 1996's *Mission: Impossible*.

Stage (standing in for the Eurotunnel) and landing on the back of a speeding train, a crashing helicopter in hot pursuit. As he often does, Cruise performed most of his own stunts. 'I was flying across the James Bond Stage at Pinewood Studios and hit a train,' he told *Film Review* magazine at the time. 'It really hurt and I didn't have to act at all.' Indeed, many old faces were returning to Shepperton just as they were at Pinewood. Eric Idle came back for his Hollywood-funded comedy *Splitting Heirs*, and found the studio considerably more active than when he was there before with *Nuns on the Run*.

Kenneth Branagh was also back for one of many return visits following his experience on *Henry V*, this time for *Mary Shelley's Frankenstein*. A sort of unofficial companion piece to Francis Coppola's recent *Bram Stoker's Dracula*, as both chose to go back to the original source novels more faithfully than previous film versions, Branagh's adaptation saw him beefed up on camera whilst handling his most ambitious production to date behind it. The actor-director cast himself as Victor Frankenstein and Robert De Niro as his Creature, alongside what was now almost becoming a regular Branagh repertory company of both actors and technicians.

'I was flying across the James Bond stage at Pinewood Studios and hit a train. It really hurt and I didn't have to act at all.'

Tom Cruise on choosing to accept an (almost) Impossible Mission

'Because this was a larger-than-life gothic story,' Branagh recalled at the time, 'it required the right kind of backdrop. Designer Tim Harvey and I agreed that what was needed was to create a world that had sort of a heightened reality. It had to be full of primary colours, full of scale and space and, where necessary, light and sunshine. Putting the story in a natural setting would not be appropriate. The only way we could maintain total control – and achieve a consistency of style and tone – was in a studio environment.'

Several large, elaborate sets were constructed at Shepperton, most notably the doctor's laboratory, which witnesses the amniotic-fluid-soaked birth of the Creature (even if KY Jelly was standing in – as usual – for said fluid).

Mary Shelley's Frankenstein was a film that disappointed on release but whose reputation has subsequently grown in stature.

The next big-budget Hollywood production to lens at Shepperton also failed to connect with the box office but is unlikely ever to be re-evaluated in a favourable way.

Kenneth Branagh attempts to build the perfect beast – directing and starring in *Mary Shelley's Frankenstein* (1994) at Shepperton.

Hot off the success of his stylish London-set crime drama *The Young Americans*, young Brit director Danny Cannon was recruited to bring Judge Dredd to the screen. Dredd, the hard-assed, no-nonsense future lawman of MegaCity One, had first appeared in 1977 on the pages of *2000 AD*, the first British comic to offer any sort of riposte to the dominance of Marvel and DC comics in the UK during the late '70s and early '80s. He was an instantly iconic figure. Whilst fans of the comic were eager for a big-screen outing for their (anti) hero, nobody was hungry for the lead role to go to Rambo. Sylvester Stallone was signed as the Judge, and being the (naturally) ego-led actor that he was, he insisted on playing the majority of the film without Dredd's face-obscuring helmet. It became, in short, not so much a Judge Dredd movie as a Stallone movie. And not one from his golden period. (It should be noted that just two years earlier, Stallone had starred in *Demolition Man*, another future cop movie, and one that seemed much more suited to his notable talents.)

'It was probably the biggest real explosion inside the 007 Stage ever and it was exactly as you see it in the film.'

Producer Iain Smith on one key element of *The Fifth Element*

Luc Besson confers with an alien creature on the set of his elaborate *The Fifth Element* (1997).

It was rapidly turning into a decade of happy returns at Pinewood. Anthony Hopkins was back, minus his hair, for *Surviving Picasso. Memphis Belle*'s Michael Caton-Jones's reworking of Frederick Forsyth's *The Day of the Jackal* – now simply *The Jackal* – marked the quick return of *First Knight*'s Richard Gere, and the slightly longer-delayed reappearance of Sidney Poitier, who had last worked at the studio in 1967's *To Sir, with Love. The Jackal* also starred Bruce Willis, who barely left the studio that year, also starring as a future flying cab driver in Luc Besson's big-budget sci-fi extravaganza *The Fifth Element*, one of Pinewood's largest-scale productions of the decade. It was produced by veteran Iain Smith, who had most recently been at the studio with *Mary Reilly*.

'*Mary Reilly* was very focused on the house and the street, so it was fairly contained, although it was large,' Smith explains. 'With *Fifth Element* we were dotted around all over the place and of course by that time we were definitely in the realm of visual effects, so we had to create New York with flying taxicabs and all that good stuff, so there was a lot of green screen. For the first time really we were using green screen as a very dominant feature in the production. But in terms of the spirit of the production it was a very different atmosphere altogether. *Mary Reilly* had a lot of tension, where *The Fifth Element*, led by the wonderful Luc Besson, was a rather joyful experience. Everybody really appreciated it and enjoyed it and I think that comes across on the screen.

Eyes Wide Shut (1999) shot for fifteen months. Taking time out to eat, here we see director Stanley Kubrick, with producer Jan Harlan and leads Tom Cruise and Nicole Kidman.

'The main set that we built on the 007 was Fhloston Paradise,' continues Smith, 'which is the space station resort that they all head off to. In particular we shot the big explosion where the Mondoshawans are out to get the fifth element and Bruce Willis, of course, springs into action and the Mondoshawans fire a rocket at him at the bar and the whole thing goes up. It was, I think, probably the biggest real explosion inside the 007 Stage ever and it was exactly as you see it in the film.'

Although the government had been making some inroads towards understanding and supporting the British film industry, it clearly wasn't fully on board yet. Mel Gibson had planned on filming *Braveheart*, his epic tale of Scottish freedom fighter William Wallace, on location in Scotland and then back at Shepperton, where the actor had worked previously giving us his Hamlet.

The production had asked for the loan of hundreds of British soldiers as period extras in the film's epic battle scenes. When the UK government said no, the Irish government – eager to lure Hollywood to its shores and employing new tax incentives to do so – offered up its own military and Gibson and Co. promptly decamped, losing Shepperton the production. (Gibson would return to the studios two years later, if only for a brief cameo in Charles Sturridge's *Fairy Tale: A True Story*.)

Shepperton may have lost William Wallace, but it still had King George III, in all his madness. Former Bond designer Ken Adam (now Sir Ken) won his second Oscar for his work on Nicholas Hytner's film of Alan Bennett's award-winning play, *The Madness of George III*, Adam described the sets he designed for the production as being basic rather than ornate, removing paintings from walls where they would once have hung, leaving the outline of them behind to suggest the King's fading memories.

Back on the subject of continued returns, Val Kilmer made his way back to Pinewood (for the first time since *Top Secret* in 1984), to revive *The Saint*, in the role of Simon Templar, which had originally made a huge star out of Pinewood's longest-standing resident, Roger Moore.

Even Moore's Bond predecessor, Sean Connery, found himself back at the studio that had made him a star, this time playing a villain. As part of the recent trend of resurrecting '60s spy TV shows for the big screen, *The Avengers* followed *Mission: Impossible* and *The Saint*, with Connery cast as Sir August De Wynter, joined by Ralph Fiennes donning the bowler of agent John Steed and Uma Thurman zipping up the catsuit of Mrs Emma Peel.

Now firmly established as the biggest movie star in the world, Tom Cruise was easily lured back to Pinewood by the opportunity to work with the legendary Kubrick. Little did he know he would be there for an unprecedented fifteen months.

The large-scale production (which also utilised some stages at Shepperton) saw production designer Stuart Craig construct an elaborate London street on Pinewood's backlot using innovative forced perspective to create a greater size than was actually built, and stage a blizzard in Pinewood's gardens during the height of summer.

But perhaps the greatest return to Pinewood during this time was that of Stanley Kubrick, who was back to shoot what was to be his final film, *Eyes Wide Shut*. Having worked at the studios only a couple of years before, Tom Cruise (now firmly established as the biggest movie star in the world) was easily lured back by the opportunity to work with the legendary Kubrick. Little did he and his then wife and co-star Nicole Kidman know that the actual shoot would drag on for an unexpected, and unprecedented, fifteen months.

And if Cruise had been a paparazzi target previously, this time, starring in an erotic thriller with his wife, press interest went through the roof, with those covered walkways back in place and the whole production covered in a veil of secrecy, something the ever-withdrawn and reclusive Kubrick insisted upon.

Bringing some fresh blood to Pinewood, amongst all the returnees, was the directing–producing team of Paul W. S. Anderson and Jeremy Bolt and their elaborate science fiction/horror hybrid *Event Horizon*. The production made excellent use of the 007 Stage to house the titular spaceship, perched on the edge of hell. 'I ended up as a weird monster, covered in prosthetics,' actor Sam Neill said of his time working on the film. 'Basically naked, with a weird pouch where my genitals had been torn away. We were shooting at Pinewood in midwinter. It was wet, cold and horrible.'

Also new to the lot was Rowan Atkinson, who brought his popular TV character Mr Bean to the big screen in *Bean: The Ultimate Disaster Movie*. Pinewood veteran Sir John Mills returned in a scene shot in the Pinewood boardroom, with the actor sitting at the head of the table where he had originally signed his first contract with J. Arthur Rank many years before.

Sir John Mills returned to Pinewood for a scene in *Bean: The Ultimate Disaster Movie* and found himself in the Pinewood boardroom where he had originally signed his first contract with J. Arthur Rank, many years before.

Luc Besson wasn't the only film-maker making use of the 007 Stage for elaborate sci-fi extravaganzas – Brit director Paul W. S. Anderson used it to – literally – open the gate to hell in space, in 1997's *Event Horizon*.

Despite a relative increase in production throughout the early part of the decade, Shepperton's future was by no means guaranteed. It became a good deal more secure, however, when a new consortium of investors, Candover Partners, signed a deal worth $28.5 million. Following on from the Kordas, the Boultings and the Lees, the studios were once again in the hands of a set of brothers, Ridley and Tony Scott, together with Neville Shulman, their long-term adviser, who took on the role of alternate director.

In the press release issued after the sale in January of 1995, the partnership stated, 'We recognised that with the right investment, the team had the broad experience, excellent worldwide experience and a proven track record needed to grow revenues and attract a greater volume of higher added volume business.'

'I have made films there for the last twenty years, so there is a historical attachment,' Ridley Scott added at the time. 'But we are also finding that American and European film companies are coming over to make movies and hope Shepperton can share in that influx of new business.'

Looking back on that move now, Ridley Scott recalls, 'I thought it was about time that Tony and I "paid back" a little of what we had enjoyed over the years at Shepperton and that we, as part of an investment group, should acquire Shepperton Studios from the Lee brothers. With the backing of Candover Investments, a young, aggressive investment company, over the next five years £37 million was invested in improvements at Shepperton. Building J and K stages, recovering buildings to create a formidable art department, then putting in animated mixing rooms. Recovering the old lawn and gardens. Shaping up the whole place. I believe we all worked so long and such hard hours so that the studio could be competitive and pleasant. And we made it precisely that.'

'I thought it was about time that Tony and I "paid back" a little of what we had enjoyed over the years at Shepperton.'
Ridley Scott and Co. take charge of Shepperton

Under the guidance of the Scotts, the studio underwent a major refit and upgrade, with old buildings finding new names in honour of the likes of David Lean, Orson Welles and, belatedly, Alexander Korda.

Shepperton favourite Kenneth Branagh was one of the first to move in under this new order, initially as an actor, taking on the role of Iago opposite Laurence Fishburne's Othello in Oliver Parker's adaptation of the Shakespeare perennial.

Branagh also brought his next two productions as director to the studio. The first of these, *In the Bleak Midwinter*, was a low-budget black-and-white comedy drama about a group of amateur actors attempting to put on a production of *Hamlet*. The second was *Hamlet* itself.

Branagh put up his own money to cover the $1 million budget of *In the Bleak Midwinter*, enlisting a cast of trusted colleagues, many of whom he had worked with before, including Richard Briers, Michael Maloney, Jennifer Saunders, John Sessions, Julia Sawalha and Joan Collins.

For *Hamlet* (which once again saw Branagh following in the footsteps of his idol Olivier, who had directed and played the lead in his version of the play – albeit at Pinewood – in 1948), the director took on a $16 million budget and an altogether more eclectic, star-driven international cast, boasting the likes of Robin Williams, Charlton Heston, Jack Lemmon, Billy Crystal and Gerard Depardieu, alongside such home-grown talent as Kate Winslet, Judi Dench, Julie Christie, Richard Attenborough, Derek Jacobi, John Gielgud, John Mills and even comedian Ken Dodd.

Charlton Heston prepares to take his bows as the Player King in Kenneth Branagh's elaborate production of *Hamlet*, shot at Shepperton Studios in 1996.

The live-action *101 Dalmatians* (1996) saw Shepperton overrun with puppies, and Glenn Close decked out in Anthony Powell's stunning costumes.

Richard Briers, Michael Maloney and Nicholas Farrell all crossed over into both of Branagh's films, although all played different roles in *Hamlet* than those assigned them in the rehearsals of *In the Bleak Midwinter*.

Branagh's take on the Bard was equally ambitious outside of its casting. Shooting in 70mm (a format not used in the UK since David Lean's *Ryan's Daughter* back in 1970), his plan was to film the entire text of Shakespeare's play, resulting in a distinctly non-commercial running time of close to four hours (over the four-hour mark if you factored in the intermission he had planned for the film's release).

Branagh's regular production designer Tim Harvey constructed an elaborate balconied state hall lined with mirrors that led to antechambers where other moments of intrigue could be played out.

At the time of production, Branagh had recently separated from his wife, actress Emma Thompson, who, as fate would have it, also ended up shooting at Shepperton.

Thompson was starring in *Sense and Sensibility*, in her own (later Oscar-winning) screenplay, adapted from Jane Austen for Taiwanese director Ang Lee. Kate Winslet appeared in both films, as Ophelia in Branagh's *Hamlet*, and as Marianne Dashwood in Thompson's *Sense and Sensibility*.

Proving unable to stay away from his old stomping ground, Sean Connery returned to Pinewood yet again, this time as both producer and star on the stylish thriller/heist movie *Entrapment*, co-starring Catherine Zeta-Jones. His friend Michael Caine was also back at the studio where he had shot *The Ipcress File* and his other Harry Palmer adventures many moons ago, for Philip Kaufman's *Quills*, a retelling of the last days of the Marquis de Sade, which saw Caine star alongside Kate Winslet and Joaquin Phoenix, with Geoffrey Rush as de Sade.

Friends, then the world's most popular sitcom, made use of the studios for a London-set special episode, and toddler TV's finest – Teletubbies TinkyWinky, Dipsy, Laa-Laa and Po – could often be seen making their way through post-production.

Television was still playing a significant part in continuing production at Pinewood. Late-'70s hit *The Professionals* was briefly revived as *The New Professionals*, a title that reflected all the originality of *The New Avengers* a decade before. Veteran sitcom *Last of the Summer Wine* continued to use the studio for its Yorkshire-set interiors, whilst various US mini-series, such as Hallmark's *20,000 Leagues Under the Sea*, were frequent visitors to the studios' facilities.

Friends, then the world's most popular sitcom, made use of the studios for a London-set special episode in its fourth season, and toddler TV's finest – Teletubbies Tinky-Winky, Dipsy, Laa-Laa and Po – could often be seen making their way through post-production.

If Pinewood was awash with Teletubbies, Shepperton found itself overrun with puppies. Disney brought their live-action remake of *101 Dalmatians* to the studio, and whilst the title of the film only allowed for just over a hundred of the breed, the puppies recruited grew at such a rate that they needed to be replaced every two weeks. As the production scoured the country for Dalmatian breeders, Shepperton found itself playing host to nearly a thousand dogs during the course of the shoot. Studio areas were constantly disinfected, as many of the dogs were too young to have had the necessary inoculations by the time they were required to make their screen debut.

Director Alan Parker has often returned to both Pinewood and Shepperton to put finishing touches to such projects as *Evita* (1996).

Human lead Jeff Daniels spent his time on set not playing with the dogs but reading the just-published anonymous political memoir *Primary Colours*, whilst Glenn Close was busy terrorising the animals as Cruella de Vil in her superb range of costumes designed by Anthony Powell.

A sequel, inevitably if not very imaginatively titled *102 Dalmatians*, was quickly put into production shortly after the initial film's huge success at the box office. Glenn Close reprised her role as Cruella and Shepperton once more found itself chock-full of puppies.

The mid '90s was a relatively happy time at Shepperton. New chairman Ridley Scott used the studio for post-production of his Demi Moore-starrer *GI Jane*, Alan Parker was ensconced putting the finishing touches to Madonna as *Evita*, and Richard Attenborough returned, this time bringing Sandra Bullock with him, for his Hemingway-based wartime romance *In Love and War*.

With British studios playing host to more and more large-budget, FX-driven Hollywood movies, the Scotts' backers, Candover Partners, bought into an on-site FX company, The Mill, with the plan of expanding it and offering productions such as the then-shooting *Lost in Space* the opportunity to have a certain amount of the effects work done on site.

Additionally, they expanded the studio further by building new J and K stages (on what was previously a car park), converting the run-down old ones (once the province of The Who) into new office space.

The rest of the decade saw a further upturn in production at Shepperton. Never a stranger, always a friend, Kenneth Branagh was back once more, this time with the notion of combining the songs of Irving Berlin, George Gershwin and Cole Porter with the words of William Shakespeare, relocating the bard into a musical version of *Love's Labour's Lost* set in the 1930s, via a series of stylised sets built at the studio.

Then Hollywood came calling on a huge scale, not once but twice, for Stephen Sommers's *The Mummy* and its sequel. The lure of H Stage to accommodate the films' mammoth sets was a deciding factor in the director choosing Shepperton.

In *Shakespeare in Love*, the exteriors of the Rose and the Globe theatres were built on the backlot, with the theatres' interiors created in lavish detail to accommodate an audience of up to 800 costumed extras.

Big-time American movie star Julia Roberts, who years before had abandoned production on *Shakespeare in Love*, was back at the studio playing big-time American movie star Anna Scott in Richard Curtis's romantic comedy *Notting Hill*, ironically around the same time Gwyneth Paltrow was taking over the role Roberts had walked away from, as *Shakespeare in Love* was finally revived. The exteriors of the Rose and the Globe theatres were built on the backlot (alongside a labyrinth of twisting, turning Elizabethan London streets), with the theatres' interiors created in lavish detail to accommodate an audience of up to 800 costumed extras.

Another period piece, this time set in the 1980s, gave Shepperton its final hit of the decade, a story that combined the bitter miners' strike of that time with a young boy's desire to dance: *Billy Elliot*.

Under his regime, Steve Jaggs saw Pinewood rebuild, upgrade and expand, with the building of two new stages (the interlinked R and S stages) and a new office facility, named the Stanley Kubrick Building. This period also saw a dramatic change to Pinewood's famed gatehouse entrance, when the iconic Rank symbol of the man with the gong was replaced by a sign that read simply 'Deluxe'. Deluxe Entertainment services came into being to bring together Rank Video Services, Rank Film Laboratories and Pinewood Studios.

Just under a year later, venture capitalist group 3i approached Ivan Dunleavy, then chief executive of VCI plc, to look into the acquisition of Deluxe.

Actor Brendan Fraser's battle against the CGI bad guys slowly comes together during the filming of *The Mummy* (1999), which made much use of the cavernous H Stage at Shepperton.

'The origin of the transaction is that I was a sort of free agent from my previous role as chief executive of VCI,' Dunleavy explains, 'and was asked by one of the venture capitalists in the City of London to look at buying Deluxe, the film laboratory part of it, from Rank. That deal didn't proceed but as part of that I noticed that there was this business called Pinewood Studios sitting underneath Deluxe in Rank's corporate empire and I said to the venture capitalists, would they mind if I attempted to buy it on my own account? And they very kindly said, no problem at all. I'd worked with Michael Grade in a previous role and was aware that he, in fact, had had a go at trying to buy Rank Film Distributors in a previous life. And we got together one morning for a cup of tea and I suggested to him that we had a crack at Pinewood Studios.'

Within two years, he and newly appointed Pinewood chairman Lord Michael Grade would approach the Scott brothers with the notion of merging Pinewood and Shepperton.

The notion to combine Pinewood and Shepperton, back just after the turn of the century in 2001, proved to be a very fortuitous one. 'The two studios have been competing for years against each other,' Michael Grade said at the time. 'In an increasingly global market this makes no sense. Together, we can enhance Britain's share of the international movie-making business.'

In the early days, those behind the merger knew it would not be easy. People needed to see that what had once been two major forces, had now become one. 'I think the challenge wasn't the transaction,' Ivan Dunleavy recalls, 'the challenge was the culture of the two businesses. Shepperton had a long and really great history of working with mainly independent film-makers and had a variety of owners over the years, strangely enough most of whom were brothers, leading up to Ridley and Tony Scott heading the consortium owning the business. Whereas Pinewood, culturally, was seen as the grand ocean liner of studios, so just merging these two activities, which had very complementary skills and experiences and assets, was a bit of a challenge to begin with.

'We had to convince people that what we wanted to do was to take the best of breed from both and really come up with a studio for the future.'

It was a challenge that Pinewood more than met as, over the following years, the biggest movies of the day came to shoot with the Pinewood Group, which, as the new century continued, became a global enterprise.

And the rest, as they say, is history.

Preparing to step out – a young Jamie Bell turns to dance in *Billy Elliot*, Shepperton's last big hit of the decade.

THE SHAPE OF THINGS TO COME

I N EARLY **2016**, DISNEY CHAIRMAN BOB IGER TOLD THE BBC 'there are five *Star Wars* films – four more with *Episode VII: The Force Awakens* – that are in varying stages of development and production. There will be more after that, I don't know how many, I don't know how often … Marvel, you're dealing with thousands and thousands of characters – that will go on forever … I think we keep raising the bar in terms of telling stories that bring them back, that excite them, that make it feel new and that is what we do for a living.'

This was good news for Pinewood, which had just played host to the production of the first *Star Wars* stand-alone film, *Rogue One: A Star Wars Story*, and would accommodate *Star Wars: Episode VIII* for most of the studio's eightieth anniversary year, and also had Benedict Cumberbatch over at Shepperton bringing Marvel's *Doctor Strange* to life, and the *Guardians of the Galaxy* transferring from Shepperton to Pinewood Atlanta Studios for their second volume.

In the space of four years, an area that was originally just a wheat field and a school building has been transformed into a studio complex housing large purpose-built stages. Pinewood Atlanta Studios now covers 700 acres of land housing eighteen large film stages. In fact, Pinewood currently has as much land in the State of Georgia as it does in the UK.

Pinewood's ideas for overseas expansion had begun in Canada in 2009, before helping to create facilities in Malaysia, the Dominican Republic and, of course, in Atlanta, where Marvel has already shot *Ant-Man*, *Captain America: Civil War* and *Guardians of the Galaxy Vol.2*.

Each of Pinewood's international locations have been carefully selected for their strategic regional importance. Malaysia, for example, is very important to the South East Asian market, the Dominican Republic works for North American projects with such close proximity to the States and is a springboard into the Latin American markets. In Atlanta, Pinewood has created a studio that has witnessed a migration from Hollywood to Georgia, proving the case for overseas expansion which is still an ongoing ambition for the studio.

CEO Ivan Dunleavy has even started to look east. 'I'd be delighted to talk about China. At this moment in time I would emphasise that all the forecasters are predicting that the Chinese box office will become the biggest box office in the

world in the next couple of years, and given everything we've said about Pinewood's ambitions for a more global stage, it absolutely makes sense for us to be exploring the Chinese marketplace.'

Part of Pinewood's plan for the future has been to provide what in essence could be looked on as bespoke film-making facilities – if you need water and an endless horizon, you go to the Dominican Republic; if you need relatively close access to Hollywood, Atlanta's your pick; if you need the scale and versatility of the studio's own rich history, you could always come back to the UK. Whatever a film-maker's needs, Pinewood sees it as its responsibility to fulfil them.

Certainly in the UK, *Star Wars* seems to have found itself a home at Pinewood.

'We had the good fortune of not only talking about one movie but several,' Lucasfilm head Kathleen Kennedy explains, 'and we're talking about building teams of talent, so it becomes a different conversation than just coming in and talking about one film. As far as pressure goes, yes, we're all under an incredible amount of pressure to deliver, but the good thing is almost every single person that comes on to these

The beginning of the new millennium has seen Pinewood Studios expanding on a global level, including building a new complex in Atlanta, Georgia, which in its first years of operation played host to Marvel's *Ant-Man* (2015) and *Captain America: Civil War* (2016).

PRECEDING PAGE: Felicity Jones leads a new team into a whole new world and a new *Star Wars* story – one that stands alone from the classic saga. *Rogue One: A Star Wars Story* shot extensively at Pinewood during 2016.

Stormtroopers – having a blast at Pinewood! *Star Wars: Episode VII The Force Awakens* (2015) took over twelve stages at Pinewood throughout their shoot in 2014.

movies is a *Star Wars* fan. They have some kind of personal commitment that they're making to the movie, and I can't say that you always get that kind of response from people on other productions. People who are working on these movies care deeply, and it's important to them and it's important to their kids and in some cases it's important to extended family members. So it just takes on a different kind of experience than I've had with most other movies I've made.'

As well as looking after such Disney-owned properties as Marvel and Lucasfilm, Pinewood have also recently played host to a string of Disney remakes and reinventions, from *Maleficent* to *Cinderella* to *Beauty and the Beast*, as well as furthering solid ties with such studios as Universal with *Snow White and the Huntsman* (and its sequel) and the Tom Cruise version of *The Mummy*.

With its relationships with these companies designed to continue forward, the future is certainly looking bright for Pinewood. But the studio does not rest on its tent-pole-related laurels.

'We're moving more and more into content. We've announced Pinewood Television, high-end drama television, as a new presence for us, which we're excited about.'

Pinewood chairman Lord Michael Grade

The studio is not solely geared to film production, as Pinewood's chairman, Lord Michael Grade, explains of Pinewood's expansion into new areas of television. 'We're moving more and more into content. We've announced Pinewood Television, high-end drama television, as a new presence for us, which we're excited about obviously. Drama is so, so important today, whether you're Amazon, Netflix, BBC, ITV, NBC, CBS; it's the big tent-pole dramas that drive your service and give you a distinctive edge. What *House of Cards* has done for Netflix, everybody's trying to do. It started with HBO and *The Sopranos*. That changed the game completely and we want to meet that market because it's a growing market.'

In addition to this planned move into high-end television drama, Pinewood has started co-financing and developing film and television, with Pinewood Pictures financing, arranging funding and distributing such movies as *Spooks: The Greater Good*, a spin-off from the hugely popular TV show that added *Games of Thrones*' Kit Harington to the already established TV cast, as well as co-funding Amazon's high-end television drama, *The Collection*.

Pinewood's foley team record sound
effects for EA Sports, *Madden
NFL 17* game. Here the team are
recording the sounds to replicate
the football players running into,
and tackling, each other.

Not all the work Pinewood has been developing has been in front of the camera, though, with considerable expansion taking place in providing additional services to productions as well as remaining home to a community of craftsmen.

Pinewood Creative, an in-house prop-making and set-building workshop, occupies one of the original parts of Pinewood, which has been the Carpenter's Mill since 1936. It services film and TV productions on and off the lot, as well as museums, exhibitions and the retail industry, and combines traditional skills and the cutting edge of contemporary tech.

One of the oldest and longest-standing residents on the lot, C & P Graphics, run by the father-and-son team of Peter and Andrew Wright, the firm was formed by Peter (who had previously worked at the studio as a signwriter) shortly after Pinewood went 'four-wall', and began his independent career by making the road signs for the studio itself.

Over the years, C & P Graphics have found themselves called upon to create signwriting from all eras and for all genres of movie, from the Dickensian times of *Great Expectations* to the modern mystical world of Marvel's *Doctor Strange*.

Pinewood in the UK has continued to expand into television production, offering facilities that call for a full studio audience, on such productions as the popular singing contest show *The Voice UK*.

Harry Pearce (Peter Firth) goes out into the cold in 2015's *Spooks: The Greater Good*, one of the first movies funded by Pinewood Pictures.

'It ebbed and flowed in those days. You'd get a rush of work for a few months and then it kind of died down. But over the years it's picked up enormously with the studio getting bigger all the time.'

Peter Wright, of the family-run C & P Graphics, who have been based at Pinewood for more than two decades

Dave Shaw, who heads up Diving Services UK out of Pinewood, is renowned in the film industry when it comes to marine services, after working on such films as *Spectre, Skyfall, Casino Royale*, the *Harry Potter* franchise and more recently Tim Burton's *Miss Peregrine's Home for Peculiar Children*. Shaw has also been hands-on in Pinewood's expansion all over the world, helping to design and build the Horizon Water Tank in the Dominican Republic. Over a four-year period, bushland on the Caribbean island became a state-of-the-art horizon water tank and a studio.

'Four years were spent going backwards and forwards designing the water facility in the Dominican Republic. Now it is up and running with a local team managing the marine facility.'

They had the latest *xXx: The Return of Xander Cage* with Vin Diesel as one of their first productions.

Dave details the specifics of the tank itself. 'The marine facility is absolutely awesome: it's a 75-by-75-metre square tank. It is 1.4 metres deep, which is the perfect depth and has a deep tank in the centre, 20 metres by 20 metres and 3.6 metres deep. There are also wave machines, tip tanks, rostrums and walkways which can be utilised for special effects.'

After his many years of supervising such activities at Pinewood and around the world, Dave is reluctant to pick any one thing he sees as being the most ambitious or challenging work – 'probably the next one', he says!

With the rise of digital, Pinewood has also adapted, providing digital content and post-production services on film productions from budgets of $1 million to $200 million. As films can shoot on the latest camera formats, or traditional 35mm film, the Pinewood team has to manage the digital medium or film process through the creative and technical workflow, creating multiple backups for long-term storage, picture editorial media and dailies creation for online review. Dailies are usually viewed by secure cloud services where members of the crew including the director, cinematographer, editor and others can view and discuss the dailies as a group. This is a far cry from the days of old.

The 65,000 sq ft Horizon Water Tank at Pinewood Dominican Republic Studios.

The world of modern computer gaming is also turning more and more to Pinewood and its varied facilities. AAA games budgets for sound post-production are on a par with film productions as the gaming experience is increasingly cinematic and immersive. So Pinewood with its background and talent can creatively bring something to the games market. However, the video game is often a very different beast to the conventional movie. Working on a film is a linear process, it has a duration of roughly two hours depending on the cut and script. Game play can be anywhere up to ten to fifteen hours, maybe more depending on the complexity of the game and the tree effect, picking your own path through virtual worlds. One of the games Pinewood has recently worked on has a number of lead character and creatures voices that have been cast, recorded and edited over an eight month period.

Although Pinewood has long been associated with some of the biggest movies in the history of cinema, that doesn't mean the Pinewood of the future will be forgetting the little guy. Alex Garland, whose low-budget *Ex Machina* beat fellow Pinewood resident *Star Wars: The Force Awakens* to the Oscar for Best Visual Effects in 2016, was only too happy to take his second film, *Annihilation*, back to the studios. Meanwhile, over at Pinewood Toronto Studios, Irish director Lenny Abrahamson

A further example of how Pinewood likes to accommodate all shapes and all sizes – Lenny Abrahamson directs Brie Larson to an Oscar win, alongside a young Jacob Tremblay in the claustrophobic *Room*, built at Pinewood Toronto Studios.

constructed his claustrophobic *Room*, leading to numerous Oscar nominations and a win for Best Actress, Brie Larson.

It's important to Pinewood as a business, as an organisation, to ensure that the smaller films have a foothold in Pinewood and Shepperton, because it's the future of the business in the UK to have home-grown product. When you look at some of the directors that are now directing the huge blockbuster movies, they started out in the UK commercials industry or television, and the young directors and producers and cinematographers and so on are all coming through. They need to start somewhere and Pinewood does everything they can to make sure that they are there to help them. Take the post-production team – one day they might be doing something as big as *Star Wars: Episode VIII* and the next day they might be helping someone finish off a short film that they're putting together for film school. Pinewood is that sort of organisation.

'One of the most important things that we work hard at,' adds Lord Michael Grade, 'is trying to ensure that the rich history of the skill base we have in the UK is maintained. That's hugely important. It's almost limitless how many big movies you can make at one time in the UK because the skill base is so huge. We've got to make sure we don't take that for granted and that we reseed the beds and do our bit for training and development and so on. That's hugely important; very, very important.'

In 2016, Bond producers Michael G. Wilson and Barbara Broccoli returned to Pinewood with the first production to use the new stages 3 and 4, *Film Stars Don't Die in Liverpool*, starring Annette Bening and Jamie Bell.

Benedict Cumberbatch prepares to expand the Marvel Cinematic Universe in a distinctly spiritual direction in 2016's *Marvel's Doctor Strange*, which saw the Marvel crew return once again to Shepperton.

Captain America found himself facing off against new Marvel recruit T'Challa, aka the Black Panther, in 2016's *Marvel's Captain America: Civil War*. This time at least he had a green screen to back him up!

As much as Pinewood has looked to expand all around the world, it has also realised that the demand for film production facilities in the UK has led to a requirement for growth at home. Back in 2007, it submitted ambitious plans to expand on land adjacent to the studio. The first concept saw a development that would incorporate permanently standing street locations, as well as housing – something that both Sir Auckland Geddes and Charles Boot would surely have approved of.

Pinewood considered a number of options for the use of the land since it was acquired. Expanding Pinewood became the primary aim and the next question was, how best do they achieve that? They successfully obtained planning permission to build new production facilities and the first phase of development was completed in June 2016; however, their first concept for the land, Project Pinewood, approached the future of the industry from a different angle. The intention of that was to create a living and working community alongside the existing studios with residential units accommodated in generic streetscapes from around the world that productions could use for location filming.

'One of the most important things that we work hard at, is trying to ensure that the rich history of the skill base we have in the UK is maintained. That's hugely important. It's almost limitless how many big movies you can make at one time in the UK because the skill base is so huge.'

Lord Michael Grade on maintaining the future of the British film industry

That idea failed to secure the necessary planning permission, but after ten years of work, planning permission was approved and the land was built on, affording the studios a grand total of five new sound stages in its first phase (with more to follow in phase 2 and 3) – as part of the Pinewood Studios Development Framework (PSDF) – alongside all the supporting workshops and offices such a facility requires. The first production to use the facilities was Michael G. Wilson and Barbara Broccoli's *Film Stars Don't Die in Liverpool*.

Producer Iain Smith's most recent movie was the multi-Oscar-winning *Mad Max: Fury Road*, and whilst that shot on location in the Namibian desert, Smith himself has kept his offices on the lot at Pinewood for many years. 'I'm on the lot. I've got my offices. I've had them here for a long time. I was at Shepperton before when Ridley moved in and wanted my office. So I moved over. But I've always kept offices here and that's where we sit and make our plans for the future.'

Smith has literally been watching the growth of Pinewood from his office window. And whilst he is delighted to see the new stages go up, he suspects five may not be enough.

'I'm watching them with a keen eye because I'd rather shoot in the UK than have to go abroad to shoot. I do believe that five stages are not enough. I think if they'd made it ten stages then they would be able to fill them all. The studio's in great shape. It's great to have Lucasfilm here and we're certainly grateful in the industry to have Pinewood leading the way. They're very much a leadership organisation.'

The last time he worked at Pinewood, Sam Mendes was given the opportunity to convert the 007 Stage into a large section of Westminster Bridge, surrounded by a 360-degree view of night-time London, for *Spectre*. It's no wonder he's looking forward to coming back.

'It was insane,' the film-maker enthuses, 'because of course you initially think, well, hang on a minute, I don't want to have to build this, why can't we just shoot on

Bond (Daniel Craig) and Madeleine
Swann (Lea Seydoux) in the Dining
Car recreated at Pinewood Studios
for *Spectre* (2015).

Westminster Bridge? The truth is, to shoot on Westminster Bridge with a crashed helicopter in flames, that's complicated in the centre of London! So you shoot what's at either end of the bridge, (those characters watching Bond) on location, and then you shoot what's happening at the centre of the bridge on the set at Pinewood. Then you blend the two using visual effects. Night shoots on location are difficult, whereas on stage we shoot it during the day, but it looks like night. Obviously one of the big gains about shooting something like that on stage is that you use people's energy better, otherwise you could be shooting forever. We'd still be shooting the movie now if it weren't for Pinewood.

'I want to praise Pinewood because I love it. It's a great place to work. It's fair to say that I'm a big fan.'

Skyfall and *Spectre* director Sam Mendes

'I want to praise Pinewood because I love it,' Mendes continues. 'It's a great place to work. I believe in it, and it's been very important to me. I think it's very interesting now that you go to the U.S. and they say, "how can we make this movie happen in England?" And of course the ideal place to do that is Pinewood partly because of the tax break, partly the level of craftsmanship available, partly the brilliant crews, partly the facilities – all of those things rolled together mean that it's pretty unbeatable. Not only that, but it's expanding. So it is fair to say that I'm a big fan.'

'It's a really exciting time,' adds *Gravity* producer David Heyman. 'There's a lot of productions coming here for a combination of reasons. One, we have brilliant people working behind the camera and in front of the camera; brilliant crews and directors and actors. We also have the tax break, which is an absolute incentive to bring people here. And we have commonality of language with the US, so again that's a reason why a lot of these films come here. It's easy, it's a great place to film, it's comfortable for actors whether they be British or American. It's a great place to work with the very best crews in the world. Great visual effects facilities, great stages, studio facilities, and all that combined with the tax break makes it a very attractive place to film. As long as that all remains in place, I think it's positive. So fingers crossed.

'We do have a responsibility to develop more home-grown films, home-grown talent,' Heyman continues. 'British crews and British actors. Some films come in here with their American cast, American director, a lot of American crew and what's great about it is it encourages the development of British talent in front of and behind the camera. That is brilliant and we need that to continue. But at the same time, I think there's a responsibility to make British films that are not just studio films, which account for a huge amount of the spend here, but also independent ones.'

Recreation of Westminster Bridge
on the 007 Stage for the climactic
moments of 2015's *Spectre*.

2016's *Rogue One: A Star Wars Story* saw George Lucas's far, far away galaxy expand its horizons with the first of a proposed series of stand-alone *Star Wars* adventures.

'For over eighty years they have always provided excellent services and facilities to many film-makers and production companies and I know they will certainly do so in the future.'

Sir Ridley Scott

Another film-maker with plans to return to the newly expanded studio is Sir Ridley Scott. 'Pinewood and Shepperton are undoubtedly among the most encompassing and professional film and television studios in the world,' Scott states. 'For over eighty years they have provided excellent services and facilities to many film-makers and production companies and I know they will certainly do so in the future. They are definitely here for the long term. Their reliability and professionalism are very important to international producers, who need studios they can totally rely on, and here they know they absolutely can.

'I have produced and directed there so often: feature films, television, documentaries, as well as advertising and commercial productions, and know I shall continue to do so. I very much look forward to working with and continuing my long association with these fine studios over many more years.'

In a world in which people should never say never again, Pinewood enters its eightieth year with a bright future ahead. *Star Wars* seems to have plenty more stories to tell – and wants the studio to help tell them.

'It seems to be shaping up to be a long-term relationship,' says Kathleen Kennedy. 'It's up to the audience, but it's our job to make the best movies we possibly can and to make them as unique, and as different, story-wise, as we possibly can. As long as the audience keeps showing up, we'll keep making *Star Wars* films.'

Kennedy may also find herself bringing *Indiana Jones* to Pinewood – if her *Star Wars* movies allow for it. 'There may not be room,' the producer laughs. 'We might end up fighting with ourselves.'

And as Bob Iger so wisely pointed out, Marvel movies will go on 'forever'.

Meanwhile Universal's new reimagined universe of their classic 1930s monster movies gears up, with *The Mummy* taking up stage space in the summer of 2016 at Shepperton, a film that sees Tom Cruise back at the studios once more, and Pinewood continuing to go from strength to strength.

As Pinewood CEO Ivan Dunleavy sums up, 'Where we are at the moment is we're the leading provider of facilities and services to the global film production industry.

We are also rapidly expanding in the world of television, notably in big TV drama, which is very similar to the way film is made, and we're making good inroads into the video games space. So we want to continue to do more of that. We want to add to the services that we provide to our customers so that we are yet more of the production partner that they depend on us to be. Where are we in ten years' time? I think the business will be building on the legacy we inherited from the great work that was done in the past.'

'Where are we in ten years' time? I think the business will be building on the legacy we inherited from the great work that was done in the past.'

Pinewood CEO Ivan Dunleavy

The first eighty years may well have been glorious. But maybe the true legacy of Pinewood will turn out to be: that was just the beginning.

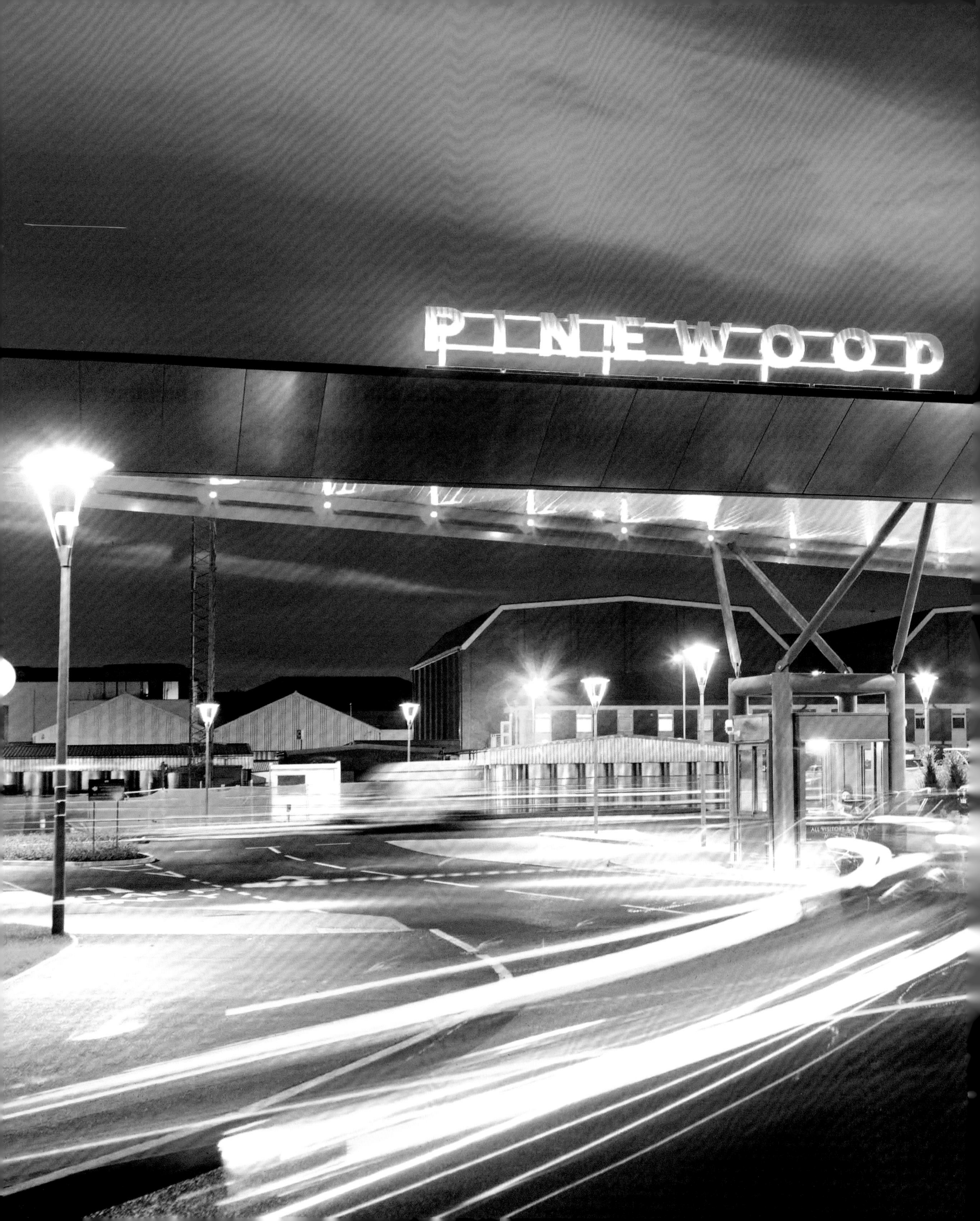
PINEWOOD

BIBLIOGRAPHY

We are deeply indebted to the following publications for their wisdom, guidance and information that helped in the construction of this book:

Bright, Morris, *Pinewood Studios: 70 Years of Fabulous Filmmaking* (London: Carroll & Brown, 2007).

Bright, Morris, *Shepperton Studios: A Visual Celebration* (London: Southbank, 2005).

Coldstream, John, *Dirk Bogarde: The authorised Biography* (London: Weidenfeld & Nicolson, 2004).

Corbett, Ronnie, *High Hopes: My Autobiography* (London: Ebury Press, 2000).

Drazin, Charles, *Korda – Britain's Only Movie Mogul* (London: Sidgwick & Jackson, 2002).

McCabe, Bob, *Dark Knights & Holy Fools: The Art & Films Of Terry Gilliam* (London: Orion, 1999).

McCabe, Bob, *Rough Guide to Comedy Movies* (London: Rough Guides, 2005).

McNab, Geoffrey, *J. Arthur Rank and the British Film Industry* (London: Routledge, 1993).

Moore, Sir Roger, *Bond On Bond: The Ultimate Book on 50 Years of Bond Movies* (London: Michael O'Mara Books Ltd, 2015).

Moore, Sir Roger, *Last Man Standing: Tales from Tinseltown* (London: Michael O'Mara Books Ltd, 2014).

Moore, Sir Roger, *My Word Is My Bond: The Autobiography* (London: Michael O'Mara Books Ltd, 2008).

Owen, Gareth, With Brian Burford, *The Pinewood Story: The Authorised Story of the World's Most Famous Film Studio* (Richmond: Reynolds and Hearn, 2000).

Owen, Gareth, *The Shepperton Story: The History of the World Famous Film Studio* (Gloucestershire: The History Press Ltd, 2009).

Perry, George, *Movies From The Mansion – A History Of Pinewood Studios* (London: Elm Tree, 1982).

Powell, Michael, *Michael Powell A Life In Movies: An Autobiography* (London: William Heinemann Ltd, 1986).

Sweet, Mathhew, *Shepperton Babylon: The Lost Worlds of British Cinema* (London: Faber & Faber, 2005).

Threadfall, Derek, *Shepperton Studios: An Independent View* (London: British Film Institute, 1994).

Trynka, Paul, *Starman David Bowie: The Definitive Biography* (London: Sphere, 2011).

Wakelin, Michael, *J. Arthur Rank: The Man Behind The Gong* (Oxford: Lion Publishing, 1996).

Wood, Alan, *Mr Rank: A Study of J. Arthur Rank and British Films* (London: Hodder & Stoughton, 1952).

– and to many newspapers, periodicals and magazines (many of which are sadly no longer with us), including –

American Cinematographer

Broadcast

Cinefantastique

Cinefx

Cinema Retro

Empire

Film Comment

Films & Filming

Film Review

Hollywood Reporter

Neon

Photoplay Film Monthly

Premiere

Screen International

Sight & Sound

Starburst

Starlog

Total Film

Many thanks to all (some of you are sorely missed.)

Page references in *italics* indicate photographs.

A

About a Boy 12
Abrahamson, Lenny 348, *348*
Abrams, J. J. 11, *11*
Academy Awards (Oscars)
 22,37, 40, 50, 93, 113, 121,
 125, 131, 156, 173, 191, 193,
 198, 202, 227, 236, 249, 255,
 264, 267, 268, 283, 294, 300,
 306, 308, 309, 311, 323, 329,
 348, 353
Ackland-Snow, Terry 241,
 274, 277, 290, 292, 294–5
Adam, Ken 164, 166, 172, 173,
 174, *178*, 179, 188, 191, 210,
 215, 323
Adams, Bryan 300, 303
Alan Parker Film Company
 223
Alas Smith & Jones 300
*Alice Through the Looking
 Glass* 12, *13*
Alien 244–5, 246–9, *247*, *250–1*,
 252, *253*, *254*, 255, 258, *259*,
 260–1, 267, 274, 300
Alien 3 300
Aliens 274, 276, *276*, 277, 278,
 278–9
Allder, Nick 255
Allen, Irving 160
Amalgamated Studios,
 Elstree 107
American Photographic
 Corps 108
Amicus 198
An Ideal Husband 125
Anderson, Gerry 191, 223,
 226, 227, 312
Anderson, Paul W. S. 324
Andress, Ursula 164, 198
Angeli, Pier 156, *156*
Anglo Amalgamated Film
 Distributors Ltd 147
Angry Silence, The 155, 156
Annihilation 348
Ant-Man 40, 338, 339
Army Film and Photographic
 Unit (AFPU) *96–7*, 99,

105–6, 108, 131
Ashcroft, Peggy 91
Asquith, Anthony 98
Atkinson, Rowan 324
Atonement 22, *24–5*, 25
Attenborough, Richard *104*,
 105, 106, 155, 156, *156*, 268,
 303, 306, *307*, 327, 330
Auger, Claudine 166, *167*
Avengers, The 323
Avengers: Age of Ultron 10,
 20, *20*, 40, 306
Ayling, Dennis 255

B

Bach, Barbara *196–7*, 198
Badejo, Bolaji 252, 255
Bain, Barbara 223
Balcon, Michael 106
Bale, Christian 12, *14–15*
Barry, John 164, 176, 235
Bates, Alan 155
Batman 4, 283, *284–5*, 286–7,
 287, *288*, 289–90, *291*, 292–3,
 292–3, 294–5, *296*, 297
Batman Begins 12, *14–15*
*Bean: The Ultimate Disaster
 Movie* 324
Beard, John 270
Beatrice, Princess 315
Beauty and the Beast 45, 341
Beaver Films 155, 156
Beetlejuice 286, 287
Bell, Jamie *334*, 335, 349, *349*
Belles of St Trinian's, The
 138, *139*
Bentley, John 202, 216, 218,
 219
Bergin, Patrick 300
Besson, Luc 320, *321*, 324
Billion Dollar Brain 179,
 182–3, 183
Billy Elliot 331, *334*, 335
Black Narcissus 113, 119,
 119, 125
Bloom, Claire 179
Bogarde, Dirk 132, *133*
Bolt, Jeremy 324
Boot, Charles 59, 60, 64, 67,
 69, 73, 78, 105, 352
Boulting, John *104*, 105,106,

129, 155, 186, 187, 188, 277,
 324
Boulting, Roy 106, 129, 186,
 277, 324
Bowie, David 216, *217*, 218,
 268, 289
Box, Betty 112, 132, *133*, 135,
 135, 138, 160
Box, John 312
Bram Stoker's Dracula 318
Branagh, Kenneth 12, 45,
 52–3, 53, *282*, 283, 300, 301,
 301, 311, 318, 319, *319*,
 326–7, 327, 328, 329, 331
Brando, Marlon 234–5, *238*,
 239, 289, 303
Brannigan 218
Braveheart 322,
Bresslaw, Bernard *148–9*,
 149, 219
Bridget Jones's Diary 12
British and Dominions Film
 Corporation 69, 78, 81
British Lion 198, 202, 216,
 219, 246
British National Films 61,
 64, 67, 99, 100
Broccoli, Albert R. 'Cubby'
 4, 17, 31, 32, 156, 160, 161,
 161, 164, 172, 173, 174, 176,
 186, *196–7*, 198, 207, 208, 210,
 210, *211*, 215, 216, 219, 273
Broccoli, Barbara 17, 172, 173,
 208, 211, 215, 273, 348, 349,
 353
Brooks, Mel 264, 267
Brooksfilms 264
Brosnan, Pierce 12
Bugsy Malone 223, *224–5*,
 225
Bullock, Sandra 22, *23*, 37,
 38–9, 40, 330
Burbage, Sir Richard 86
Burgin, Dr Leslie 64, *64*, 70,
 73, 75, *75–6*
Burton, Richard 140, 179
Burton, Tim 12, *18–19*, 19,
 286–7, *287*, *288,* 289, 290,
 293, 294, 295, *296*, 297, 300,
 346

C

C & P Graphics 343, 346
Cain, Syd 208, 264
Caine, Michael 179, *182–3*,
 183, 308, 329
Cameron, James 274, 276,
 276, 278, *278–9*
Campbell, Ivor 87
Campbell, Judy *114–115*, 115
Candover Partners 324, 330
Cannon, Danny 315, *315*, 320
Capra, Frank 108
Captain America: Civil War
 10, 22, 40, *41*, 338, 339, 352,
 352
*Captain America: The First
 Avenger* 40
Cardiff, Jack 113, 121
Caridia, Michael *130*, 131
Carry On Abroad 140, *148–9*,
 149
*Carry On at Your
 Convenience* 140
Carry On Camping 140, *141*
Carry On Cleo 140, *142–3*
Carry On Columbus 147, 151,
 303, *304–5*, 305
Carry On Constable 140
Carry On Cowboy 140, *146*,
 147
Carry On Emmannuelle 140,
 147
Carry On England 147
Carry On Henry 140, *150*, 151
Carry on Matron 69
Carry On Nurse 140
Carry On Sergeant 138, 140
Carry On Series 69, 112, 138,
 140, *141*, *142–3*, *144–5*, 145,
 146, 147, *148–9*, 149, *150*,
 151, 179, 207, 210, 303,
 304–5, 305 *see also under
 individual movie name*
Carry On Spying 140, 179
Carry On Teacher 140
Carry On Up the Khyber 140
Carstairs, John Paddy 131
Casino Royale (1967) 160,
 198, *199*, *200–1*, 201
Casino Royale (2006) *26–7*,
 27, *272–3*, 273, 346

Caton-Jones, Michael 320
Chaplin 156, 306, *307*
Chariots of Fire 268
Charlie and the Chocolate Factory 12
Children's Film Foundation 126
Chilton, Ed 227
Chitty Chitty Bang Bang *172*, 172, 173, 174, *174–5*
Christie, Julie *326–7*, 327
Cimino, Michael 264
Cinderella 10, 12, 45, *52–3*, 53, 341
Cinematograph Films Act (1927) 98, 100
Clark, Candy 216, *217*
Clarke, Arthur C. 188, 192
Cleese, John 312, *313*, 315
Cleopatra 140, *142–3*, 179, 290
Clockwork Orange, A 193
Clooney, George 37, *38–9*
Close Encounters of the Third Kind 248, 252
Close, Glenn 328, *328*, 330
Cole, George 138
Collection, The 341
Collins, Joan 126, 327
Collins, Lewis 264
Colonel Blood 91
Coltrane, Robbie 280, *281*, 283
Columbia Pictures 187, 188
commercials/advertising 246, 348, 360
Company of Wolves 268, 270, *271*, 290
Company of Youth (Rank Charm School) 126
Connery, Sean *4*, 6, *158–9*, 161, 162, *162–3*, 164, *165*, 166, *167*, 176, *177*, 179, 198, 207, 264, 303, 312, 323, 329
Connor, Kenneth 138, 140, *149*
Coppola, Francis 318
Corbould, Chris 31
Corfield, John 61, 64, 67, 69, 99-100
Cornfeld, Stuart 267
Cortez, Ricardo 64, *64*
Costner, Kevin 300, *302*, 303

Craig, Daniel 7, 27, *28*, 32, *33*, 33, 354, *354–5*
Craig, Stuart 267, 312, 323
Cribbins, Bernard 147
Crown Film Unit 105
Cruise, Tom *4*, *194*, 195, 270, *298–9*, 301, 309, 311, 312, 315, *316–17*, 318, 322, *322*, 323–4, 341, 361
Crying Game, The 306, *306*
Cuarón, Alfonso 37, *38–9*
Cumberbatch, Benedict 338, *350–1*, 352
Curse of the Pink Panther, The 267–8
Curtis, Richard 308, 331
Curtis, Tony *206*, 207

D
D&P Studios Ltd 100
Dahl, Roald 12, 172
Dale, Jim 147
Dalton, Timothy 216
Dance, Charles 300
Daniels, Jeff 330
Danson, Ted 315
Dark Knight, The 10, 16
Dark Shadows *18–19*, 19
Davidson, Jaye 306, *306*
Davies, John Howard 113, *118*, 119
Davis, John 151
Davis, Judy 264
Day Lewis, Daniel 308, 311
DC Comics 286, 320
De Laurentiis, Dino 252, 258
De Niro, Robert 318
Deakins, Roger 27
Dean, Basil 91
Deeley, Michael 219
Deighton, Len 179
Deluxe Entertainment 331, 335
Dench, Judi 309, *309*, 327
Deneuve, Catherine 268
Denham Film Studios 93, 100, 105, 108, 112, 121, 128, 129
Depp, Johnny 19, *19–20*
Deutsch, Oscar 100, 107, 151
Diamonds Are Forever 176,

177, 179, 198, 207
Diana, Princess 312, 315
Die Another Day 12
Diesel, Vin 346
Disney 11, 12, 45, 50, 126, 132, 135, 161, 173, 286, 329, 338, 341
Disney, Walt 45, 132, 135
Diving Services UK 22, 25, 346
Doctor in the House 132, *133*, 135
Doctor Strange 40, 338, 343, *350–1*, 352
Donner, Richard 12, 16, 218, 230, *232*, 233–4, 235, 239, 240, 241
Dors, Diana 126
Douglas, Kirk 186
Douglas, Robert 75, *75–6*, 78, *79*
Downey Jr, Robert 306, *307*
Doyle, Sir Arthur Conan 268, 269
Dr No 160, 161, 164, *165*, 166, 172, 176, 188, 191, 207
Dr Strangelove or: How I Learned to Stop Worrying and Love the Bomb 4, 166, *184–5*, 187–8, *189*, *190*, 191
Dragonslayer 135
Drake of England 91
Dunleavy, Ivan 11, 12, 21, 331, 335, 338–9, 341, 361

E
EA Sports 342
Eady Levy 280
Ealing Studios 106
Eaton, Shirley 132, *133*, 162 *162–3*, *168–9*, 169
Edwards, Blake 267
Elephant Man, The 4, *262–3*, 264, *266*, 267, 268,
Ellers, Sally 64, *64*, 75, *75*
Elstree Studios 58, 59, 64, 67, 69, 70, 78, 81, 107, 191, 218, 230, 274
EMI 198, 219, 246, 258
Empire Strikes Back, The 227
Entrapment 329
EON Productions 17, 160,

172, 198
Eraserhead 264, 267
Eugenie, Princess 315
Evans, Chris 40, *41*
Event Horizon 324, *325*
Evita 330, *330*
Ex Machina 45, 46, *46–7*, 50, 348
Eyes Wide Shut 194, 195, *322*, 322, 323–4

F
Fairy Tale: A True Story 322
Fallen Idol, The 80, 81
Feldman, Charles 198
Ferretti, Dante 309
Fiennes, Joseph 308, *310*, 311
Fiennes, Ralph 323
Fierce Creatures 312, *314*, 315
Fifth Element, The 320, *321*
Film Stars Don't Die in Liverpool 348, 349, *349*, 353
Films Act (1960) 100
Fincher, David 300
First Knight 312, 320
Firth, Peter *344–5*, 345
Fish Called Wanda, A 312, 315
Fitzgerald, Geraldine 64
Flash Gordon 258
Fleming, Caspar 173
Fleming, Ian 160, 161, 164, *165*, 172, 173, 198
Flicker Film Productions 86
Forbes, Bryan 155, 156, *156*
Ford, Harrison 11, *11*, 45, 300
Four Weddings and a Funeral 308, *308*
Francis, Freddie 98, 267
Frears, Stephen 312
Freeman, Morgan 300, *302*, 303
Frenzy 100, *101*, 103, 202
Friends 329
Fröbe, Gert *4*, *158–9*, 161, 166, 173
From Russia With Love 164, 166
Full Metal Jacket 193, 195, 274, *275*
Funeral in Berlin 179
Furst, Anton 270, 290, 292–3, 294, 295, 297

G

Gandhi 156, 268
Garland, Alex 46, *46–7*, 348
Gassner, Dennis 32
Gaumont-British 56, 89, 91, 100, 107
Geddes, Sir Auckland 58–9, 67, 78, 105, 352
George, Peter 187
Gere, Richard 312, 320
GI Jane 330
Gibson, Mel 300, 322
Gielgud, John 301, *301*, 327
Giger, H. R. 247, 249, 251, 252, 255
Giler, David 248
Gilliam, Terry 218–19, *220–1*, 221, 270
Gilliat, Sidney 108, 112, 138
Glegg, Graham 61
Glover, Brian 300
Goldfinger 4, 22, *158–9*, 161, 162, *162–3*, 166, *168–9*, 169
Goldwyn, Samuel *90*, 91
Grade, Michael 11, 335, 341, 352, 353
Grainger, Stewart 115, *115*
Granada Television 268
Grant, Hugh 308, *308*
Gravity 10, 22, *23*, 37, *38–9*, 40, 356
Gray, Sally 115, *115*
Great Expectations 112–13, *113*, 116, *116–17*, 126, *127*, 343
Great St Trinian's Train Robbery, The 138
Green for Danger 112
Green, Guy 156, *156*
Grenfell, Joyce 138
Groves, Peter 115, *115–16*
Guardians of the Galaxy 30, *30*, 338; *Vol. 1* 40; *Vol. 2* 40, 338
Guber, Peter 286
Guinness, Alec 113, *118*, 119, 216
Guitens, Bert 64, *65*

H

Hackers 311

Hackman, Gene 234
Hamilton, Guy 166, 204, *204–5*, 208, *209*, 230, 233
Hamlet (1990) 300, 322
Hamlet (1996) *301*, 301, *326–7*, 327–8, 329
Hammer Films 140, 267
Hand, David 126
Handmade Films 283
Harington, Kit 341
Harlan, Jan 322, *322*
Harrison, Rex 98
Harry Potter franchise 37, 40, 346
Harry, Prince 312, 315
Hartnell, William 138
Harvey, Tim 318, 328
Hawtrey, Charles 138, 140, *144–5*, 145, *148–9*, 149
Heatherden Hall, Buckinghamshire 22, 58, *58*, 59–60, *60*, *62–3*, 64, 67, 87, 264
Heaven's Gate 264
Helpmann, Robert 172, *172*, 173
Henry V 12, *282*, 283, 318
Heyman, David 37, 40, 356, 360
Hickox, Douglas 268
Hill, Walter 248
Hiller, Wendy 98, *99*, 99, 100, 202, *202*
Hills House, Buckinghamshire 93
History of the World, Part I 264
Hitchcock, Alfred 100, *101*, *102–3*, 103, 202, 207, 297
Hobson, Valerie *114–15*, 115
Hodges, Mike 258
Hopkins, Anthony 267, 320
Hound of the Baskervilles, The 268, 269, *269*
Howard, Cyril 280, 309
Howard, Leslie 98
Hudis, Norman 140
Hudson, Hugh 246, 268
Hugo 36, *36*
Hunger, The 268

Hunt, Gareth *222*, 223
Hunter, Ian 160
Hurd, Gale Anne 274
Hurt, John *4*, 202, *202*, 251, *251–2*, 255, *266*, 267
Hyams, Peter 264, 277, 280, *280*

I

Idle, Eric *221*, 221, 280, *281*, 283, 318
Iger, Bob 338, 360
In Love and War 330
In Search of the Castaways 132
In the Bleak Midwinter 326–8
Independent Producers Ltd 108, 112, 119, 121, 128, 129
Indiana Jones franchise 10, 360
Intelligence Men, The 179, *180–1*, 181
Interview with the Vampire 309, 311
Into the Woods 10
Ipcress File, The 179, 329
Ireland, Jill 126, 155
Iron Lady, The 50, *50*
Iver Heath, Buckinghamshire 11, 59, 83, 98, 105, 147, 172

J

Jabberwocky 219, *220–1*, 221
Jack Ryan 300
Jackal, The 320
Jacobi, Derek *326–7*, 327
Jacques, Hattie 138
Jaggs, Steve 309, 331
James Bond series *4, 6, 7*, 10, 12, 17, 21, 22, *26–7*, 27, 31, 32, *32–3*, 33, 37, 49, 131, 140, 158–72, *158–9*, *161*, *162–3*, *165*, *167*, *168–9*, *170–1*, 172, 173, *196–7*, 204, *204–5*, 207, 208, *209*, 210, *210*, 211, *211*, *212–13*, *214*, 215, 216, 219, 230, 239, 264, 270, 274, 283, 295, 309, 354, *354–5*, 356,

357, *357*, 361 *see also under individual movie name*
James, Sid 140, *146*, 147, *148–9*, 149, *150*, 151
John, Rosamund *114–15*, 115
Johnson, Brian 191, *192–3*, 223, 227, 248–9, 252, 255
Jolie, Angelina 50, *51*, 311–12
Jones, Felicity *336*, 339
Jordan, Neil 268, 270, 290, 306, *306*, 309, 311
Judge Dredd 315, *315*, 320

K

Kanin, Garson 108
Kaufman, Philip 329
Keaton, Michael 284–5, 286, 287, 288, 289, 294
Kennedy, Kathleen 10, 45, 339, 341, 360
Kenny, Chris 290
Kent, Jean 115, *114–15*
Kerr, Deborah 113, 119, *119*
Kidman, Nicole 195, 322, *322*, 323–4
Kilmer, Val 323
Knightley, Keira 22, *24–5*, 25
Korda, Alexander 69, 89, *90*, 91–3, *93*, 95, 100, 107, 112, 121, 125, 126, 128–9, 218, 227, 277, 324, 327
Korda, Vincent 92, 121, 125
Korda, Zoltan *88*, 89, 92, 93
Kristel, Sylvia 147
Kubrick, Stanley 166, 186–8, *187*, *189*, *190*, 191, 192–3, *194*, 195, 274, *275*, 277, 280, 322, *322*, 323, 324, 331
Kurtz, Gary 223, 227

L

L-Shaped Room, The 155
Ladd, Alan 156, 160
Lamont, Peter 273, 274
Landau, Martin 223, *226*, 227
Larson, Brie 348, *348*
Last of the Summer Wine 329
Laughton, Charles 69, 93, *94–5*, 95

Launder, Frank 108, 112, 138
Lawson, Wilfrid 64
Lazenby, George 176, *176*, 207
Lean, David 89, 108, 112, 113, 116, *116–17*, *118*, 119, 126, *127*, 128, *128*, 129, 202, 210, 211, 215, 246, 277, 326, 328
Lee International Studios, Shepperton 277, 327
Lee Studios 277, 327
Lee, Ang 329
Lee, Barry 277, 327
Lee, Christopher 126
Lee, John 277, 327
Legend 216, 270, *272*, 273–4, 311
Leigh, Vivien 98, 128
Les Misérables 44, *44*, 50
Lester, Richard 235, 239, 241, 303
Levin, Dr Drury 59
Lightbox, the 37
Lithgow, John 280, *280*, 289
Little Shop of Horrors 274
Littleton Park Estate 86–7, *87*
Live and Let Die 204, *204–5*, 207–8
Living Daylights, The 216
Llewelyn, Desmond 164
Lloyd's of London 105
Loch Ness 315
London Films 89, 92–3, 100, 107, 121, 128
London Melody 78, *79*, 81, *82–3*, 83
London Town 112
Lost in Space 330
Loudon, Norman 86, 87, 89, 91
Love Actually 12
Love's Labour's Lost 331
Lubezki, Emmanuel 37
Lucas, George 10, 223, 227, 359
LucasFilm 10, 45, 339, 341, 353, 356
Lumley, Joanna *222*, 223
Lynch, David 264, *266*, 267

M
MacDowell, Andie 308, *308*
Macnee, Patrick *222*, 223
Madden NFL 17 (computer game) 342, *342*
Madness of George III, The 323
Madonna 330, *330*
Maibaum, Richard 164, 166, 172
Major Barbara 105
Maleficent 45, 50, *51*, 311–12, 341
Mamma Mia 48–9, 49
Man for All Seasons, A 198, 202, *202*
Man of the Moment 131
Man Who Fell to Earth, The 216, *217*, 218, 258
Man with the Golden Gun, The 208, *209*
Man with Your Voice, A 81
Mankiewicz, Tom 233, 235
Marriott, Moore *114–15*, 115
Marshall, Frank 10
Marvel Studios 10, 30, 40, 41, *41*, 306, 320, 338, 339, 341, 343, 352, 360
Mary Reilly 312, 320
Mary Shelley's Frankenstein 318, 319, *319*
Mastery of Christ, The (short film) (later retitled *Mastership*) 56, 61
Mastrantonio, Mary Elizabeth 300
Maude, Arthur 87
McCallum, David 155
Meddings Magic Camera Company 295
Meddings, Derek 241, 295
Memphis Belle 320
Mendes, Sam 22, 31, 32, 33, *33*, *34–5*, 35, 37, 354, 355, 356, 357
MGM Borehamwood, Elstree 191, 198, 219
Mill, The 330
Miller, Larry *304–5*, 305

Mills, Hayley 132, 155, 156, *157*
Mills, Juliet 156, *157*
Mills, John 113, *113*, 115, *114–15*, 324, 327
Mission: Impossible 223, *298–9*, 301, 315, *316–17*, 318, 323
Modern Age, The 126
Monkhouse, Bob 138
Moonraker 160, 215–16
Moore, Demi 330
Moore, Roger *4*, 21, 61, 160, *196–7*, 198, 204, *204–5*, *206*, 207–8, *209*, *214*, 215, 216, 219, 240, *240*, 267, 268, 323
Morden, Lieutenant Colonel Grant 59, 70, 87
More, Kenneth 129, 151, 155
Morecombe, Eric 179, *180–1*
Motion Picture Association of America (MPAA) 125, 126
Mower, Patrick 147
Mummy, The (1999) 331, *332*, 333, *333*
Mummy, The (2017) 341, 361
My Darling Daughter 156

N
National Film Fund Company 128
Neagle, Anna 78, *79*
Neame, Ronald 108
Neill, Sam 324
New Avengers, The 222, 223, 329
New Professionals, The 329
Nicholl, Commander Sir Edward 86–7
Nicholson, Jack 289, 294
Night to Remember, A 22, 151, *152–3*, *154*, 155
Niven, David 160, 198, 200–1, *201*
Nolan, Christopher 12, 16, 176
Norman, Monty 164
Norton, Richard 69, 73, 78, 81, 100, 105
Nostromo 249, 255, 277
Notting Hill 331

Nuns on the Run 280, *281*, 283, 318

O
O'Bannon, Dan 248, 249
Oberon, Merle *90*, 91, *94*, 95
Octopussy 216, 240
Odeon 100, 107
Oliver! 198, 202, *203*, 218–19
Oliver Twist 113, *118*, 119, 128, *128*, 202
Olivier, Laurence 283, 327
Omen, The 218, 230
On Her Majesty's Secret Service 176, *176*
One of Our Aircraft is Missing 124, 125
One of Our Dinosaurs is Missing 135
101 Dalmatians 328, *328*, 329–30
Oscars *see* Academy Awards
Othello 326
Outland 264, 277
Owen, Gareth 306

P
Palace Pictures 270
Palache Report 107–8
Paltrow, Gwyneth 308, 331
Parallel 9 303
Parker, Alan 223, *224–5*, 225, 246, 330
Parker, Oliver 326
Pascal, Gabriel 98, 105
Passage to India, A 277
Patriot Games 300
Peck, Gregory 218, 230
Perisic, Zoran 239–40
Persuaders!, The 21, *206*, 207
Peters, Jon 286
Pevsner, Tom 273
Phoenix, Joaquin 329
Pickens, Slim 188, *189*
Pinebrook Films 100
Pinewood Studios *362–3*
  A Stage 32, 239
  Albert R. Broccoli 007 Stage 12, *13*, 16, *16*, 31, 32, *34–5*, *48–9*, 49, *52–3*,

216, 230, *231*, 235, 239, 270, *272*, 273, 274, 293, 300, 312, 315, *316–17*, 318, 320, 322, 324, *325*, 356, 357, *357 see also* 007 Stage
at 80 8–53
Atlanta base, U.S. 21, 31, 40, 41, *41*, 338, 339, *339*, 341
Batman franchise revitalises 283, 286–97 *see also under individual movie name*
bespoke filming-making facilities, plan to provide 339
birth of 56–83
Bond franchise, as home of 16–17, 22, 31 *see also under individual movie name*
Bond franchise, effect of emergence upon 158–83 *see also under individual movie name*
Carpenter's Mill 343
Chinese market and future of 338–9
closed (1938) 105
co-financing and developing of film and television 341, 343, *343*, 361
commercials/advertising and 246, 348, 360
construction and design of 67, *68*, 69–70, *71*, 73
Deluxe Entertainment and 331, 335
Denham Studios combined with to form D&P Studios Ltd 100
destination of choice for film-making community 10–11
digital and 346–7
Dominican Republic, expansion into 21, 338, 339, 346, 347, *347*
eightieth anniversary 338

fiftieth anniversary 277
financial difficulties 128, 151, 207, 227, 229, 241, 280, 283
first films produced at 81, 98–9
'four-wall' (productions provide own crews), transition to 280, 283, 343
future of 339, 358, 360–1
gatehouse entrance 331
Heatherden Hall and 22, 58, *58*, 59–60, *60*, 62, 64, 67, 87, 264
Horizon Water Tank 346, 347, *347*
live television broadcasts 75, *76–7*, 303
Malaysia, expansion into 21, 338
Marvel Studios, relationship with 10, 30, 40, *41*, 306, 320, 338, 339, 341, 343, 360
merger with Shepperton 11, 12, 16, 335 *see also* Shepperton Studios name 67
007 Stage 12, *13*, 16, *16*, 31, 32, *34–5*, *48–9*, 49, *52–3*, 210, *210*, 211, *212–13*, 215, 216, 230, *231*, 235, 239, 270, *272*, 273, 274, 293, 300, 312, 315, *316–17*, 318, 320, 322, 324, *325*, 356, 357, *357 see also* Albert R. Broccoli 007 Stage
opening of 64, *64*, 72, 73, *74–5*, 78, 81, 98
overseas expansion 10, 21, 31, 40, *41*, 338–9, *339*, 341, 346, 347, *347*, 348, *348*
Paddock Tank 19, 22, *26–7*, 27, *28–9*, 32, 37, *154*, 155, 166, *167*, 216, 241, 312
Pinewood Creative 343
Pinewood Group and 30, 40, 335

Pinewood Pictures 341, 345
Pinewood Studios Development Framework (PSDF) 353
Pinewood Studios Limited formed 67
Pinewood Television 341, 343, 361
post-production team 330, 346, 347, 348
post-war emergence of key film-makers and performers and 110–57
Project Pinewood 353
Q Stage 31
'quota quickies' and 98, 100
R Stage 331
Rank and *see* Rank, J. Arthur
rebuild, upgrade and expansion under Jaggs 331
recent success of 10–53
Richard Attenborough Stage 50
S Stage 331
smaller (low budget) movies at 45, 46, *46–7*, 60, 348, *348*
South Corridor *68*, 69
Stage 3 349
Stage 4 349
Star Wars franchise and future of *336–7*, 338, 339, 340, *340*, 341, 348, *358–9*, 359, 360 *see also* *Star Wars* franchise *and under individual movie name*
Superman franchise as saviour of 230–41 *see also under individual movie name*
television production and 75, *76–7*, 198, 223, 223, 227, 300, 303, 312, 329, 341, 343, 348, 360, 361
thirtieth anniversary 198

Toronto Studios 21, 338, 348, *348*
twenty-first anniversary 69
UK skill base/UK talent and film, works to maintain and develop 348, 352, 353, 360
Underwater Stage 22, *23*, *24–5*, 25
unit system 70
video games and 342, *342*, 347, 361
water filming, leader in 21–2, *23*, *24–5*, 25, *26–7*, 27, *28–9*, 346, 347, *347*
World War II and *96–7*, 99, *104*, 105–6, 108, *109* *see also under individual film-maker and movie name*

Pitt, Brad 12, 309
Polish Air Force Film Unit 106
Postlethwaite, Pete 300
Powell, Anthony 328, 330
Powell, Michael 108, 113, 119, 121, *124*, 125, 128–9, 246
Pressburger, Emeric 108, 113, 119, 121, *124*, 125, 129
Primary Colours 330
Private Life of Henry VIII, The 69, 91, 92–3, *94–5*, 95
Private Life of Sherlock Holmes, The 312
Professionals, The 264, 329
Prometheus 255, *256–7*
Prudential Building Society 100
Psycho 297
Pygmalion 98–9, *99*

Q
Queen 258
Quills 329
'quota quickies' 98, 100

R
Raiders of the Lost Ark 16
Rambaldi, Carlo 252, 255

Rank, J. Arthur *4*, 45, *54–55*, 56, *57*, 58, 60-61, 64, 67, 69, 81, 98, 99, 100, 105, 107–8, 112, *114–15*, 115, 119, 121, 125–6, 128, 129, 132, 135, 151, 202, 324, 331, 335

Rank Organisation, The 45, 100, 107, 129, 138, 147, 151, 155, 227, 331, 335

Rapace, Noomi 255, *256–7*

Rattigan, Terence 98

Raymond, Jack 64, *64*

Red Dwarf 300

Red Beret, The 156, 160, 164

Red Shoes, The 119, *120*, 121

Redford, Robert 12, 233, 234

Reed, Carol 56, *57*, 64, *64*, *74–5*, 75, *80*, 81, 108, *122–3*, 123, 125, 202, *203*, 246

Reeve, Christopher *228–9*, 230, *232*, 233, 234, 239–40, *240*, 286

Reis, Spencer 67

Religious Film Society 56

Reunion 87

Reynolds, Kevin *302*, 303

Rice, Anne 309, 311

Richardson, Ian 268

Richardson, Joely 315

Rickman, Alan 300

Rigg, Diana 176, *176*

Ringwood, Bob 294

Ritt, Martin 179

Roberts, Julia 308, 312, 331

Robin Hood 300

Robin Hood: Prince of Thieves 300, *302*, 303

Roc, Patricia *114–15*, 115

Roeg, Nicolas 216, *217*, 218, 258

Rogers, Peter 138, 140, *146*, 147, 151, 303

Rogue One: A Star Wars Story 4, 45, *336–7*, 338, 339, *358–9*, 359

Rollerball 219

Room 348, *348*

Rosenberg, Max 198

Rowling, J. K. 40

Royal Air Force Film Unit *104*, 105–6, 155

Ruggles, Wesley 112

Rush, Geoffrey 329

Russell, Ken 179, *182–3*, 183

Rutherford, Margaret 98, 132, *132*

S

Saint, The 323

Salkind, Alexander 230, 233, 234, 235, 238, 239, 241, 286, 289

Salkind, Ilya 230, 233, 234, 235, 241, 286, 289

Saltzman, Harry 160, 161, *161*, 172, 176, 179, *182–3*, 183, 198, 215, 219

Sanders of the River 88, 89, 93

Sanders, George 98

Scheider, Roy 280, *280*

Scofield, Paul 202, *202*, *282*, 283

Scorsese, Martin 36, *36*, 277

Scott, Ridley 11, 216, 246–9, *247*, *250–1*, 251, 252, *254*, 255, *256–7*, 258, *259*, 270, 273, 274, 276, 303, 324, 326, 327, 330, 335, 353, 360

Scott, Terry 138

Scott, Tony 11, 12, 246, 268, 324, 327, 335

Searle, Ronald 138

Second World War (1939-45) *4*, 87, *96–7*, 99, *104*, 105–9, *109*

Secret Garden, The 303

Sellers, Peter 186–7, 188, 198, 267, 268

Selznick, David O. 108, 125

Sense and Sensibility 329

Seven Days to Noon 129

Seymour, Michael 252

Shakespeare in Love 308, 309, *309*, *310*, 311, 312, 331

Shaw, Dave 22, 25, 346

Shaw, George Bernard 98, 105, 234

Shearer, Moira *120*, 121

Shepperton Studios 10, 30, *30*, 36, 37, *38–9*, *84–5*, *88*, *89*, 179, 202, *203*, 328, *328*, 329

Alexander Korda involvement with 69, *88*, 89, *90*, 91–2, 93, *93*, 95, 107, 121, 125, 128, 129

Alien as saviour of *244–5*, 246–9, *247*, *250–1*, 252, *253*, *254*, 255, 258, *259*, *260–1*, 267, 274

Amicus and 198

Barry Spikings as chairman 219

Beaver Films and 155, 156

becomes a facility for hire and asset stripped (1974) 218

Bentley acquires 202, 216, 218, 219

birth of 84–7, *84–5*, 87, *87*

Boulting Brothers and 106, 129, 187, 188

British Lion and 198, 202, 216, 219, 246

Candover Partners acquire 324, 327, 330

David Lean and 89, 112, 129, 202, 277

EMI partnership 219, 258

expansion of 129

financial difficulties 198, 202, 216, 218, 227

H Stage 191, 216, 218, 247, 248, *250–1*, 251, 273, 277, 331, *332*, 333, *333*

Harry Saltzman offer for 219

J Stage 246, 327, 331

K Stage 246, 327, 331

Kenneth Branagh and 12, 53, 283, 311, 318, 319, *319*, *326–7*, 327, *328–9*, 331

Lee brothers and 277, 327

Littleton Park Estate and 86–7, *87*

merger with Pinewood 11, 12, 16, 335

opening of 87

opens after World War II 112

'quota quickies' and 98

refurbishment and upgrading 277, 327, 331

Ridley Scott and *244–5*, 246–9, *250–1*, 251, 252, 253, *254*, 255, 258, *259*, 270, 276, 324, 327, 330, 353

Shepperton Studios Action Committee 216

Sound City Film Producing and Recording Studios and *84–5*, 87, *87*, 89, 91, 98, 106

Stanley Kubrick and *184–5*, 186, 187, *187*, 188, *189*, *190*, 191, 192–3, 277

The Who/Rampart Company acquires part of 246, 277

World War II and 105, 106–7, 112

see also under individual film-maker and movie name

Shulman, Neville 11, 324

Shusett, Ronald 248

Sign of Four, The 268

Sim, Alistair 138, *139*

Simmons, Jean *114–15*, 115

Sims, Joan 140, *148–9*, 149

Skyfall 10, 22, 27, *28–9*, 31, 32, *34–5*, 35, 346, 356

Sloan, James 69

Smith, Iain 312, 320, 322, 353

Snow White and the Huntsman 341

Softley, Ian 311

Sommer, Stephen 331

Song of the Plough 89

Sony 31, 40

Sound Barrier, The 129

Sound City Film Producing and Recording Studios *84–5*, 87, *87*, 89, 91, 98, 106

Southern, Terry 187

Space 1999 223, *226*, 227, 312

Space Precinct 312

Spectre 31, 32, 33, *33*, *34–5*, 346, 354, *354–5*, 356, 357, *357*

Spengler, Pierre 230, 239

Spielberg, Steven 252
Spikings, Barry 219
Splitting Heirs 318
Spooks: The Greater Good 341, *344–5*, 345
Spy Game 12
Spy Who Came in from the Cold, The 179
Spy Who Loved Me, The 196–7, 198, 208, 210, *211*, *212–13*, 215, 216, 235
Stallone, Sylvester 233, 315, *315*, 320
Star Wars franchise *4*, *8–9*, 10, 11, *11*, 16, 22, 40, *42–3*, 45, 218, 223, 227, 230, 247, 248, 258, 270, *336–7*, 338, 339, 340, *340*, 341, 348, *358–9*, 359, 360 *see also under individual movie name*
Star Wars: A New Hope 218, 223, 227, 230, 247, 248, 258, 270
Stars Wars: The Force Awakens 4, *8–9*, 10, 11, *11*, 22, *42–3*, 45, 338, 340, *340*, 348
Stewart, Hugh 106, 131
Streep, Meryl *48–9*, 49, 50, *50*
Subotsky, Milton 198
Supergirl 241, *242–3*, 292
Superman: The Movie 4, 12, 16, 216, 227, *228–9*, 230, *231*, *232*, 233, 234–5, 236, *236–7*, *238*, 239–41, 286, 289, 295
Superman II 241
Superman III 241
Superman IV: The Quest for Peace 241
Surviving Picasso 320
Swiss Family Robinson 132
Sword and the Rose, The 132

T

Tale of Two Cities, A 138
Talk of the Devil 56
Talking Feet 87
Taylor, Elizabeth 140,
Teletubbies 329

television production 75, *76–7*, 198, 223, *223*, 227, 300, 303, 312, 329, 341, 343, 348, 360, 361
Thatcher, Margaret 50, 280
Third Man, The 122–3, 123, 125
39 Steps, The 138
Thomas, Gerald 138, 140, 147, 151, 303, 304–5, *305*
Thomas, Ralph 112, 132, 135, *135*, 138, 140, 147, 151
Thompson, Emma 328–9
Thorn EMI 258
3i 331
Three Men in a Boat 91
Thunderball 166, *167*
Thurman, Uma 323
Tomkins, Les 290
Tovey, Noel 50
Trail of the Pink Panther, The 267
Trouble in Store 131, 132, *132*
True Glory, The 108, *109*
Trumbull, Douglas 191
Tucker, Christopher 267
Turn of the Tide 61, 64
20th Century Fox 40, 223
2010 277, 280, *280*
20,000 Leagues Under the Sea 329
2001: A Space Odyssey 187, *187*, 188, 191, 192–3, 223, 247, 248, 277

U

United Artists 69, 81, 160, 215, 264
Universal Studios 10, 31, 108, 341, 361
Unsworth, Geoffrey 236, *236–7*
Up in the World 110–11, 113, *130*, 131
Ustinov, Peter 108

V

Van Dyke, Dick 173
VCI plc 331, 335
Veidt, Conrad 91
Vertigo 297

View to a Kill, A 214, 215, 216, 273
Vikander, Alicia 46, *46–7*
Voice, The 343, *343*

W

Walker, Norman 64
Wallis, Wing Commander Ken 172
Wandering Jew, The 91
Warner Brothers Studios 12–13, 31, 286–7, 300, 309
Warwick Films 160
Watch Beverley 87
Watling, Jack *104*, 105
Wayne, John 218
Weaver, Sigourney *254*, 255, 258, 300
Weintraub, Sy 268, 269
Welland, Colin 268
Welles, Orson 64, 123, *122–3*, 125, 198, 246, 264, 326
Whistle Down the Wind 155, 156
Who, The 246, 252, 258, 277, 331
Who Dares Wins 264, *265*
Widmark, Richard 264
Wilcox, Herbert 73, 81
Wilder, Billy 312
William, Prince 312, 315
Williams, Kenneth 138, 140, 147, *148–9*, 149
Williams, Robin 289, 327
Willis, Bruce 320, 322
Wilson, Harold 126, 215,
Wilson, Michael G. 17, 27, *28–9*, 172, 208, 215, 273, 283, 349
Windsor, Barbara 140, *141*, *148–9*, 149, *150*, 151, 179
Winslet, Kate 327, 329
Wisdom, Norman *4*, 106, *110–11*, 112, 113, 129, *130*, 131, 132, *132*, 138
Wise, Ernie 106, 179, *180–1*, 181
Wombling Free 227
Woolf, C. M. 100, 107
Working Title 12
Worton Hall 121, 129

Wright, Andrew 343, 346
Wright, Peter 346

X

xXx: The Return of Xander Cage 346

Y

You Only Live Twice 170–1, 172, *178*, 179
Young Americans 320
Young and Innocent 100, *102–3*, 103, 202
Young, Terence 164
Yule of Bricket Wood, Lady 61, 67, 69, 99–100

Z

Zeffirelli, Franco 300
Zeta-Jones, Catherine 329
Zinnemann, Fred 202, *202*
Zucker, Jerry 312

ACKNOWLEDGEMENTS

We would like to thank the staff, the filmmakers, the talent in front of and behind the camera, the Pinewood community in the UK and worldwide, friends and family and clients, past and present for their contributions, recollections, humour and history, and for helping to make Pinewood and Shepperton Studios such magical places.

Legends have been created and dreams have been brought to life in stepping through our iconic gates and this book is a celebration of an amazing eighty years.

Particular thanks are extended to the following interviewees, without whom, this book could not have been produced:

Terry Ackland-Snow
Nigel Bennett
Barbara Broccoli
Martin Campbell
Michael Gambon
Terry Gilliam
David Godfrey
Lord Michael Grade of Yarmouth CBE
David Heyman
Brian Johnson
Neil Jordan
Kathleen Kennedy
Sam Mendes
Sir Roger Moore
Laurens Nockels
Ann Runeckles
Sir Ridley Scott
Dave Shaw
Andrew M. Smith
Iain Smith
Nick Smith
Noel Tovey
David Wight
Michael G. Wilson
Peter and Andrew Wright

AUTHOR'S NOTE

The very first time I was ever on a film set was at Pinewood Studios. And it was way back in 1977. The father of my best friend at school, Greg Smith, was a film editor for the likes of *The Prisoner* and *The Sweeney* and would occasionally take people off to a club at Pinewood that held special sneak screenings of upcoming movies that had been shot there. Thus it was that at the tender age of ten or so, I found myself watching *The Spy Who Loved Me* weeks before it came out, and afterwards wandering the lot and discovering the smashed-up yellow taxi cabs that had recently crashed into an immovable Superman.

Finding ourselves at the recently inaugurated 007 Stage – and knowing enough to know that if the red light outside wasn't lit it meant they weren't filming (plus, it was ten o'clock at night) – myself and my mate Greg climbed the covered stairway to try and peak through the doors … and were promptly caught by a security guard. Who, much to our amazement, unlocked the doors and took us for a late-night walk around Superman's Fortress of Solitude.

I almost fell into the water tank (couldn't swim at the time) as I advanced curiously to the dark patch in front of me, stopping just inches before the edge when I caught the reflection of the lights above on the surface below – just before I was about to fall in.

I know I shouldn't say this in this day and age of incredible health, safety and security – but thank God for security guards as lax (or as kind) as that man, that night. He may well have changed my life.

As I went on to write books, articles, reviews of movies, even a couple of actual movies, and more, it is likely that first trip to Pinewood was in many ways a formative experience.

I was there many times again in the mid to late '90s working with Mark Kermode (whatever happened to him?) on the late, lamented BBC Radio One show *Clingfilm*.

The opportunity to write this book brought me back there once again and I have to report – security is not what it used to be!

In terms of this particular book, there are, as ever, a number of people to thank. I am as ever in the moral and emotional debt of the wonderful publisher that is Trevor Dolby, and those at Preface, and Penguin Random House. For sterling work (and stamina) I applaud Lizzy Gaisford; for pics, company and shared bottles of wine, I am more than grateful to picture researcher Felicity Page; for some

pics and some more shared bottles of wine back in the early days (which seem so long ago now!), huge thanks also to Mel Haselden. And to David Eldridge for pulling it all together at the end. As always the staff and resources of the BFI library provided a tower of strength in the early days of this project.

The entire team at Pinewood and in particular huge thanks to Rachel Hooker, Fern Colao, Noel Tovey, Ivan Dunleavy and his team at the studio.

Of the many people who contributed along the way, I am indebted, amongst others, to Sir Ridley Scott, Kathleen Kennedy, Barbara Broccoli, Michael G. Wilson, Sam Mendes, Martin Campbell, Neil Jordan, the great Brian Johnson, David Heyman, the very generous Lord Grade of Yarmouth CBE, (I called him 'Michael'), Terry Ackland-Snow, Iain Smith and Sir Roger Moore, who took the time to be as witty and eloquent as he always is.

On a personal note, as ever I am indebted – both figuratively, and sometimes literally – for peace, love and understanding (and what's so funny about that?) to a number of people, who this time include Michael Pierson, Paul Gillion, Yusuf Khan, the Archibalds – Glenn, Vicky and Oscar (my official biographer, BTW) – Rob Churchill, Dave Battcock, Lucy Armitage, Mark Kermode, Paddy Hogan, Bernadette Chapman, Andy Gilbert and Jenny Kenmure (that's one more sale guaranteed!), Katie Griffiths, Terry Gilliam, John Cleese and the collective blast from the past that is, and indeed was, Susannah Cartwright, Heidi Erbrich, Nikki Sved, Mark Dickey-Collas, Josie Le Grice, Gerry Lynch, Richard Ashton, Brendan Clarke, John Davidson and Sam Jones – wow, that was a night! (Next time, it'll probably be a funeral!)

Thanks as ever to Lucy Merritt, and the wonder that is Teddy!

And – as ever, for always, for everything, and piles o' stuff on top – all my love to Jessie and Jack, still two of the best people I know.

Only ever really been inspired by four things in life. Movies. Pop music. And Jessie. And Jack. And I love them all very dearly … Oh, and Prince … And Robin Williams … And The Beatles, obviously … When I said 'four', well …

Bob McCabe
Somewhere in 2016
Formerly of This Parish

IMAGE CREDITS

Every reasonable effort has been made to contact all copyright holders, but if there are any errors or omission, we will insert the appropriate acknowledgement in subsequent printings of this book.

p.6 Danjaq/EON/UA/The Kobal Collection, p.7 Photograph by Greg Williams

CHAPTER 1: pp.8-9 © Lucasfilm Ltd./Bad Robot/True North Productions/Walt Disney Studios/REX/Shutterstock, p.11 © Lucasfilm Ltd./Bad Robot/True North Productions/Walt Disney Studios/REX/Shutterstock, p.13 Peter Mountain/Warner Bros./REX/Shutterstock, pp.14-15 Warner Bros./D.C. Comics/REX/Shutterstock, p.16 Courtesy of Universal Studios Licensing LLC/©2015 Everest Film Holdings, LLC, p.17 Universal/REX/Shutterstock, pp.18-19 Warner Bros./REX/Shutterstock, p.20 Marvel Studios/Walt Disney Studios Motion Pictures/Maidment, Jay/REX/Shutterstock, p.23 Warner Bros/REX/Shutterstock, pp.24-25 Focus Features/REX/Shutterstock, pp.26-27 2006 © Danjaq LLC and United Artists Corporation. All rights reserved., p.28 Danjaq/EON Productions/REX/Shutterstock, p.29 © Anderson & Low, p.30 Marvel Enterprises/Marvel Studios/Moving Picture Company/REX/Shutterstock, p.33 Columbia/EON/Danjaq/MGM/REX/Shutterstock, pp.34-35 © Anderson & Low, p.36 Gk Films/REX/Shutterstock, pp.38-39 Warner Bros./REX/Shutterstock, p.41 © Marvel Studios/Photos 12/Alamy Stock Photo, pp.42-43 © Lucasfilm Ltd./Moviestore collection Ltd / Alamy Stock Photo, p.44 Courtesy of Universal Studios Licensing LLC/©2012 Universal City Studios Productions, LLLP, pp.46-47 Dna Films/Film4/REX/Shutterstock, pp.48-49 Courtesy of Universal Studios Licensing LLC/©2008 Universal Pictures Company, p.50 Film 4/REX/Shutterstock, p.51 Walt Disney Studios/REX/Shutterstock, pp.52-53 Jonathan Olley/Walt Disney Pictures/REX/Shutterstock

CHAPTER 2: pp.54-55 Ronald Grant Archive, p.57 Everett Collection/REX/Shutterstock, p.58 Fred Morley/Fox Photos/Hulton Archive/Getty Images, p.60 Photo © Pinewood Group, p.62 AF archive/Alamy Stock Photo, p.63 Photo © Pinewood Group, p.64 J. Smith/Fox Photos/Getty Images, p.65 Fred Morley/Fox Photos/Hulton Archive/Getty Images, p.66 Fred Morley/Fox Photos/Hulton Archive/Getty Images, p.68 Photo © Pinewood Group, p.71 Photo © Pinewood Group, p.72 Photo © Pinewood Group, pp.74-75 J. Smith/Fox Photos/Hulton Archive/Getty Images, pp.76-77 Popperfoto/Getty Images, p.79 General Film Distributors/REX/Shutterstock, p.80 Bert Hardy/Picture Post/Getty Images, pp.82-83 Ronald Grant Archive

CHAPTER 3: pp.84-85 Photo © Pinewood Group, p.87 Photo © Pinewood Group, p.88 Korda/REX/Shutterstock, p.89 Photo © Pinewood Group, p.90 Imagno/Getty Images, p.93 Hulton Archive/Getty Images, pp.94-95 Hulton Archive/Getty Images

CHAPTER 4: pp.96-97 © IWM (H 30987), p.99 Moviestore Collection/REX/Shutterstock, p.101 Bob Dear/AP/PA Images, pp.102-103 Gainsborough/Gaumont-British/REX/Shutterstock, p.104 Popperfoto/Getty Images, p.109 Courtesy Everett Collection/REX/Shutterstock

CHAPTER 5: pp.110-111 ITV/REX/Shutterstock, p.113 Stanley Sherman/Express/Getty Images, pp.114-115 PA Images, pp.116-117 ITV/REX/Shutterstock, p.118 ITV/REX/Shutterstock, p.119 ITV/REX/Shutterstock, p.120 Baron/Getty Images, pp.122-123 Haywood Magee/Picture Post/Hulton Archive/Getty Images, p.124 British National/REX/Shutterstock, p.127 Nat Farbman/The LIFE Picture Collection/Getty Images, p.128 Popperfoto/Getty Images, p.130 Popperfoto/Getty Images, p.132 Bert Hardy/Picture Post/Getty Images, p.133 REX/Shutterstock, p.134 Baron/Getty Images, p.135 REX/Shutterstock, pp.136-137 British Lion/REX/Shutterstock/Reed, Ted, p.139 Popperfoto/Getty Images, p.141 Mirrorpix, pp.142-143 20th Century Fox/REX/Shutterstock, pp.144-145 Mirrorpix, p.146 Carry On Cowboy, Film Copyright © 1966 StudioCanal Films Ltd. All Rights Reserved/REX/Shutterstock, pp.148-149 ©1999 Credit:Topham Picturepoint, p.150 ITV/REX/Shutterstock, pp.152-153 ITV/REX/Shutterstock, p.154 ITV/REX/Shutterstock, p.156 Ronald Grant Archive, p.157 PA Images

CHAPTER 6: pp.158-159 Moviestore Collection/REX/Shutterstock, p.161 Paul Popper/Popperfoto/Getty Images, pp.162-163 Paul Popper/Popperfoto/Getty Images, p.165 Danjaq/EON/UA/REX/Shutterstock, p.167 Danjaq/EON/UA/REX/Shutterstock, pp.168-169 GOLDFINGER © 1964 Danjaq, LLC and Metro-Goldwyn-Mayer Studios Inc. All rights reserved. All Rights reserved, pp.170-171 You Only Live Twice © 1967 Metro-Goldwyn-Mayer Studios Inc. and Danjaq, LLC. All rights reserved., p.172 Warfield/United Artists/REX/Shutterstock , pp.174-175 Chitty Chitty Bang Bang © 1968 Danjaq,LLC and United Artists Corporation. All rights reserved, p.176 Mondadori Portfolio via Getty Images, p.177 Moviestore Collection/REX/Shutterstock, p.178 Eon Productions © 1967 Danjaq,LLC and United Artists Corporation. All rights reserved, pp.180-181 Keystone/Hulton Archive/Getty Images, pp.182-183 Mirrorpix

CHAPTER 7: pp.184-185 Hawk Films Prod/Columbia/REX/Shutterstock, p.187 MGM/Stanley Kubrick Productions/REX/Shutterstock, p.189 Hawk Films Prod/Columbia/

3 5 7 9 10 8 6 4 2

Preface Publishing
20 Vauxhall Bridge Road
London SW1V 2SA

Preface Publishing is part of the Penguin Random House group of companies
whose addresses can be found at global.penguinrandomhouse.com.

Text copyright © Pinewood Group Limited, 2016

First published by Preface Publishing in 2016

www.penguin.co.uk

A CIP catalogue record for this book is available from the British Library.

ISBN 9781848094864

Design by Two Associates

Printed and bound by Graphicom, Italy

Penguin Random House is committed to a sustainable future for our business,
our readers and our planet. This book is made from Forest Stewardship Council®
certified paper.

FSC